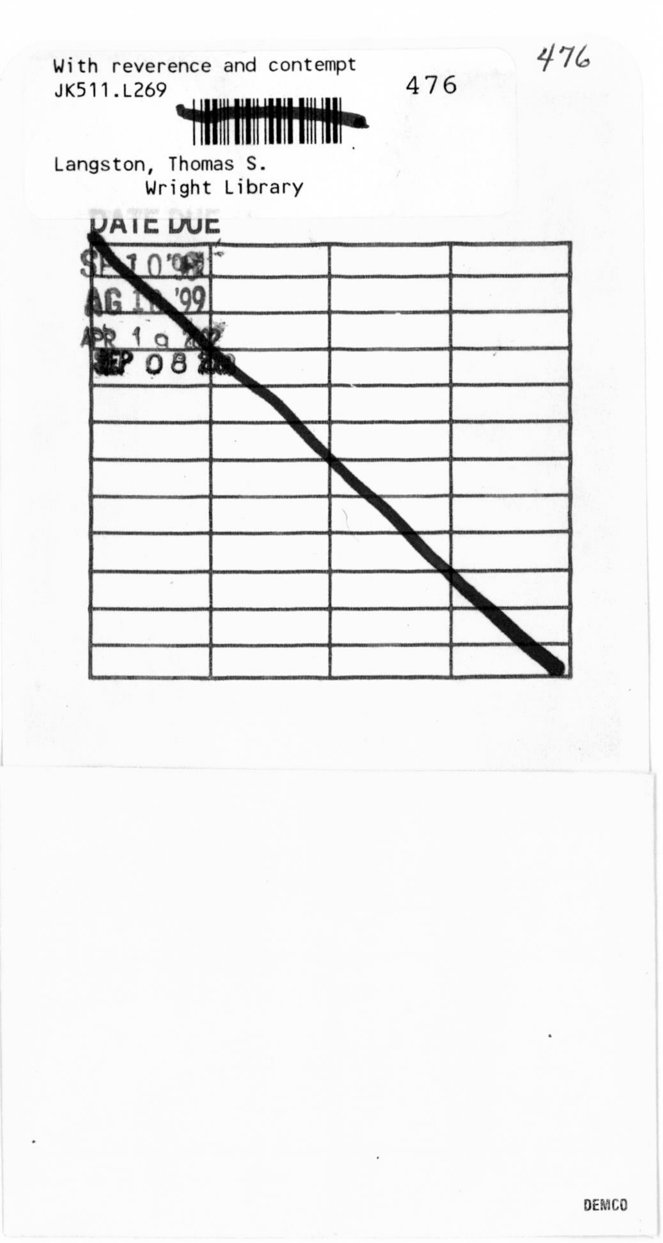
With reverence and contempt
JK511.L269
476
Langston, Thomas S.
Wright Library
DATE DUE
DEMCO

With Reverence and Contempt

INTERPRETING AMERICAN POLITICS

MICHAEL NELSON, SERIES EDITOR

The Logic of Lawmaking: A Spatial Theory Approach
Gerald S. Strom

The Institutional Presidency
John P. Burke

Regulatory Politics in Transition
Mark Allen Eisner

Executive Privilege: The Dilemma of Secrecy and Democratic Accountability
Mark J. Rozell

With Reverence and Contempt: How Americans Think about Their President
Thomas S. Langston

The Two Majorities: The Issue Context of Modern American Politics
Byron E. Shafer and William J. M. Claggett

THOMAS S. LANGSTON

With Reverence and Contempt

HOW AMERICANS THINK ABOUT THEIR PRESIDENT

The Johns Hopkins University Press

Baltimore and London

Printed in the United States of America on acid-free paper
04 03 02 01 00 99 98 97 96 95 5 4 3 2 1

The Johns Hopkins University Press
2715 North Charles Street
Baltimore, Maryland 21218-4319
The Johns Hopkins Press Ltd., London

Library of Congress Cataloging-in-Publication Data
will be found at the end of this book.
A catalog record for this book is available from the British Library.

ISBN 0-8018-5016-9

FOR MARY

CONTENTS

FOREWORD

WITHIN HOURS OF PRESIDENT JOHN F. KENNEDY'S ASSASsination on November 22, 1963, a small army of political scientists fanned out across the country to study the public's reaction to what had happened. Remarkably, they discovered that most Americans were displaying the classic symptoms of grief, symptoms that otherwise appear only at the death of a close friend or family member. People reported that they "didn't feel like eating," were "nervous and tense," and "felt dazed and numb." Combing through the historical record, scholars discovered that similar emotional outpourings seem to have accompanied the deaths in office, whether by assassination or natural causes, of all presidents, whether they were popular or not. The murder of William L. McKinley, for example, prompted a "universal spasm of grief . . . from end to end of the land"; after Warren G. Harding died in bed, "Jewish leaders compared Harding with Moses dying before he reached the Promised Land"; and Abraham Lincoln's assassination was met with an endless series of comparisons to the crucifixion of Christ.

Clearly the relationship between the American people and the presidency is a complex one. As Thomas Langston argues in this book, the relationship can only be seen plainly through the lenses of historical and cultural analysis. During the course of more than two centuries, American political culture has formed around several axioms, which are properly understood, according to Langston, as "fables." These axioms include such beliefs as "God is on our side," "The president is a crusader for freedom," "The president symbolizes America's commitment to democracy," and "When extraordinary action is necessary, presidents must take the lead."

From this congeries of cultural axioms, the presidency–and thus every president–emerges as an icon, which Langston defines in general as a "symbolic representation of something sacred or magical" and in particular as a "stylized symbol of our nation's deepest commitments and ideals." Drawing extensively from the presidencies of George Washington, Thomas Jefferson, Woodrow Wilson, Franklin D. Roosevelt, Harry S. Truman, John F. Kennedy, Lyndon B. Johnson, George Bush, Bill Clinton, and, especially, Andrew Jackson, Abraham Lincoln, and Ronald Reagan, Langston demonstrates that this icon is, oxymoronically but nonetheless empirically, a democratic priest-king.

As priest, Langston argues, the president is expected "to make meaningful the lives of the people," presiding over a civil religion that rests on the belief that "God has assigned to the American people a special role in the unfolding of His plan for humanity."

As king, the president is expected to exercise powers of prerogative. The English political philosopher John Locke defined these as the right–and duty–"to act according to discretion, for the public good, without the prescription of law, and sometimes even against the law."

The democratic element in the presidential icon, which sits uncomfortably alongside the hierarchical roles of priest and king, is that the president somehow must represent the people as a whole and, at the same time, be one of them.

Langston concludes that the relationship between the people and the president is dysfunctional–the former overload the latter with excessive and contradictory expectations that make the presidency an "implausible office," if not an impossible one. "The public, in this relationship, is encouraged to be passive but insistent, hopeful yet despairing," in a word, childish. The president, all too often, ends up as either "a tragic or a sinister figure." In the final chapter, Langston offers some proposals for reform which are intended to recast the dysfunctional relationship between the American people and their presidents.

Michael Nelson

PREFACE AND ACKNOWLEDGMENTS

THIS BOOK CAME TO BE WRITTEN IN THE USUAL WAY. AN author was invited to pitch a book on ideas and the presidency to an editor. With the help of others (more on this in a moment), a plan for the manuscript emerged. For such an exciting topic, this is an unfortunately boring story. I wish, rather, that I might say I found inspiration in the drawings of Saul Steinberg. In one of his profoundly humorous sketches, Steinberg, known chiefly for his *New Yorker* covers, depicts an American Last Supper. Seated side by side are George Washington, the Easter Bunny, Abraham Lincoln, Santa Claus, and the Statue of Liberty. A Thanksgiving turkey struts like a peacock before the assembled diners. The American presidency, Steinberg suggests, is a magical institution. Like Santa Claus and the Easter Bunny, presidents are expected to give things to people which they do not have to pay for. Like all of the nonhuman members of the party, furthermore, presidents are icons: symbolic representations of something sacred or magical. They are stylized symbols, that is, of our nation's deepest commitments and ideals. This is true, furthermore, of all our presidents, not just the Washingtons and Lincolns among them.

Consider Bill Clinton, the man from Hope. He had not even had time to select his own furnishings for the Oval Office before *Newsweek* proclaimed "The Age of Clinton" on the cover of a special commemorative issue (January 1993). The *Newsweek* cover also announced, as one of the magazine's lead stories, "Fifty Americans: What I Want from Clinton." For the president to have his "age," he was going to have to give things to people–a great many things, to a great many people. The wish lists of the *Newsweek* Fifty included the silly, appoint a secretary of entertainment; the prosaic, lift the ceiling on the amount social security recipients can earn before age seventy; and the banal, remember that raising taxes makes my life harder, understand that art matters. Mostly, though, people asked for affirmation. A family man wanted Clinton to stand for family values; a gay man wanted Clinton to advance the freedom of homosexuals; a presumably tolerant woman from Brookline, Massachusetts, wanted the president to "demand tolerance" of the rest of the nation; a high-tech entrepreneur wanted Clinton to launch a national science adventure; and a minister "would ask that he create a sense of optimism." A nine-year-old boy captured well the iconic quality of what people want from their president. "America," he asked, meaning the president, "can you help my daddy get his farm back?" The president is not just another political placeholder; to many Americans, he *is* America.

The new president had himself, in part, to blame. He had accepted the Democratic nomination in a speech proclaiming the renewal of Americans' mystical bond with providence and one another. What Clinton offered, he said, was a "New Covenant–a solemn agreement between the people and their government, based not simply on what each of us can take but on what all of us must give to our nation."[1] The New Covenant, Clinton explained, would once again make America a nation in which "there is no them; there is only us. One nation, under God, with liberty, and justice for all" (229). And what would we accomplish through our newfound spiritual strength, through a commitment "to be Americans again"? "Scripture says," Clinton answered, "[that] our eyes have not yet seen, nor our ears heard, nor our minds imagined what we can build" (230).

Covenant, of course, is a biblical idea. Scholars of religion speak, as did the Puritan settlers of the New England colonies, of covenants of grace, obligation, redemption, works, and nations. The last is the type that Clinton harked back to. According to Reformationist doctrine, human salvation is an expression of God's mercy. Since all men and women are fallen creatures, no one deserves to be saved. God saves nonetheless, but he does so sparingly. Only those communities in which "saints administer the laws according to the covenant" stand a chance of redemption.[2] Because, however, the true believer could never really be certain of anything but his or her own sinfulness, there developed within the covenanted communities of New England a desperate search for signs of God's favor. The urgent "necessity of doing something," Perry Miller writes, gripped the people of the covenant (ibid.). Americans are still, it seems, intent on "doing something" to assuage the fear that they have not been chosen after all. Who better to lead the nation in the grips of such doubt than a self-proclaimed "change agent" with a fondness for quoting Scripture?

In making his way to the presidency, then, President Clinton exploited imagery and ideas that have been part of the culture of America since before it *was* America. The idea that ours is a God-favored country is one of the most enduring themes in our national history. Its influence on presidents is one of the central subjects of this book. But there are other ideas, too, that have clothed our presidential icon, and I examine some of them as well, looking into their origins, development, and consequences from George Washington's time to our own. Many Americans believe, for a further example of the significance of ideas to the presidency, that a president should be a crusader for freedom. When President Clinton came into office, he quickly discovered just how complicated demands for freedom can become for a president. By focusing in his first weeks in office on gay rights in the military, the president affirmed the faith of some supporters but affronted the beliefs of others. How was the president to balance the demands of homosexuals to be free from military exclusion against the desire of many heterosexual soldiers to be "free" from government compulsion to live in close quarters with persons presumably so different from themselves?

What is a president to do? A more conventional analysis might ask how a president, given popular expectations of deliverance and redemption through his leadership, might best maneuver so as to maximize his power? My approach is different. I am concerned not so much with whether individual presidents win or lose but with how they play the game: with rules that reward wishful thinking on the part of the public and invite our presidents to deceive us.

If this last statement sounds polemical, that is all right, for I think of this book as a hybrid, a polemical argument. As a polemic, it has as much bite as I could give it without diminishing its seriousness. As an argument, I intend for the book to withstand, and even benefit from, a critical, objective reading. It has been composed with due regard, that is, for all standard academic conventions, except those that dictate a bloodless writing style. As a final note, the book is intended for that chimerical figure the general reader, though I believe it will be of interest as well to scholars and students of the presidency, of American studies, and of the history of American political thought.

If my book reaches any of these audiences, I will owe the credit to the many people who helped me think through and improve my manuscript. Michael Nelson, Richard Pious, Nicol Rae, and David Steiner read the entire manuscript, and I benefited greatly from their criticisms and advice. Henry Tom at the Johns Hopkins University Press also read the manuscript, and he again helped me clarify my aims as well as my prose. Chapter One draws in part from an article that was published in *Presidential Studies Quarterly*, and I would like to thank the journal's editor, R. Gordon Hoxie, for his kind permission to reprint passages from that article. Michael Lind has discussed with me many of the arguments put forth in this book, and I am grateful for his unstinting generosity with his own ideas, several of which I have almost surely appropriated as my own. Walter Dean Burnham and Peter Berger, finally, commented on some early ruminations along these lines, and I thank them for their encouragement.

The book was begun during a year I spent as a John M. Olin postdoctoral fellow at the Institute for the Study of Economic Culture at Boston University. It is my pleasure to thank the foundation, the institute, and the institute's director, University Professor Peter Berger, for the opportunity to begin this project in such a stimulating intellectual environment. The book was completed during a semester's leave from Tulane University. Obviously, none of these institutions or individuals bears any responsibility for whatever flaws remain, nor should their assistance imply agreement with what I have written.

It is conventional at this point to beg the forgiveness of one's family. But with all this help and time off, I managed to complete this book without neglecting or abusing my wife and children. This makes it all the more enjoyable to thank them–Mary, Jessica, and Taylor–for sharing a life in which, thankfully, the writing of books is but a part.

With Reverence and Contempt

INTRODUCTION

THE AMERICAN PRESIDENCY IS THE CREATION OF TWO centuries of reflection. Ironically, after devoting so much thought to the subject, the American people have decided to be governed by a veritable priest-king, the most atavistic of executives. As priest, the president is expected not only to lead the government but to make meaningful the lives of the people who constitute his congregation. As king, the president is encouraged to assert prerogative powers, including the authority to send American troops into combat, irrespective of the Congress's constitutional monopoly over declarations of war. The office's seemingly inescapable religious and royal associations have been conjoined, furthermore, with the broad acceptance of the idea that the president, to be a good democrat, must represent within the government the people as a whole. These ideas are among the intellectual supports of the contemporary presidency. When viewed in their appropriate historical contexts as well as with respect to their implications for politics and policy in the 1990s, they may be understood for what they are: highly problematic propositions with consequences for civil society and government.

The presidency, it is sometimes alleged, is an impossible institution. That, as the Reagan administration's legislative and diplomatic victories attest, is not true. Rather than impossible, the presidency is highly implausible. The institution's unlikely synthesis of religious, royalist, and democratic visions leads to unresolved and destructive tensions in public expectations of the office. President George Bush, as an icon of democracy, flattered and cajoled the populace, eating pork rinds (but not broccoli), playing upon racial fears, and grousing about the privileges of Congressmen. In his kingly capacity, Bush sent the nation to war on the basis of his independent judgment of the interests of the United States and commanded the troops who took captive a foreign head of state (see Chapter Five, below). That the president took these steps without exciting broad fears of a return to the "imperial presidency" of the Nixon years makes Bush's actions more, not less, disturbing. As pontifex maximus, finally, Bush consecrated and rallied support for his exercise of prerogative powers by exploiting the deeply compelling imagery of the American civil religion. The fight in the gulf, Bush insisted, was not for oil, or even to restore a favorable balance of power to a vital region. It was, rather, for "a big idea–a new world order, where diverse nations are drawn together in common cause to achieve the universal aspirations of mankind." Only by fighting this war, Bush implied, could America be true to itself as the "beacon of freedom in a searching world."[1]

This, it seems to me, is a strange way to conduct the affairs of government. Because we insist that occupants of the White House be democratic, like us, we tempt presidents to speak to us of the pork on a pig's back rather than in our government's budget and otherwise to flatter us to distraction. Because we routinely grant to presidents prerogative powers that rest more comfortably on the shoulders of kings, presidents sometimes act first and consult the public (and Congress) later. When they do explain their kingly actions, finally, they often choose to do so in words befitting a celestial, rather than a secular, leader. Sometimes, the result is to mask the plain and simple motivation behind a presidential decision and to brand dissent as heresy. If these impressions are accurate, then we could benefit from rethinking the combination of ideas which undergirds the contemporary presidency. But first, we have to understand how we thought ourselves into our present situation, which is what I principally hope to accomplish in this book.

INTELLECTUAL PRECEDENTS

My work draws upon that of others. Writers from several academic disciplines have offered major historical and interpretive analyses of the presidency. Bruce Miroff, Kathleen Jamieson, Garry Wills, and Barbara Kellerman are among the scholars who have contributed to our understanding of the executive office's meaning within American political thought and culture. Stephen Skowronek, Sidney Milkis, and Jeffrey Tulis have published important works that use explicitly historical methods to explore the relationship between the presidency and the people.[2]

These works exemplify what is worthwhile in two trends in political science: the turn toward history and toward interpretation. Political science early in this century was the partner of history. This was to the benefit of both disciplines. Political science's attention to institutions and decision making suggested useful topics for historical inquiry. The historical discipline's insistence on treating the past with respect opened vast territories for rigorous inquiry into the principles, both normative and empirical, of political action.[3] As Michael Nelson has observed, the lack of historical vision that not long ago characterized the study of the presidency by American political scientists led to the promulgation of theories of the institution which had embarrassingly short lives. When a strong president was in office, leading scholars of the presidency, including Thomas Cronin, Marcus Cunliffe, and Arthur Schlesinger Jr., described the office as overly strong. When a weak president followed, presidential observers, including Godfrey Hodgson and Richard Pious, emphasized the institution's alleged weakness.[4] The turn toward history has helped to correct this tendency to generalize on the basis of recent events.

The turn toward interpretation in political science is part of a multidisciplinary revival of interest in culture with a small *c*. The interpretive disposition is well described by anthropologist Clifford Geertz:

> It has dawned on social scientists that they did not need to mimic physicists or closet humanists or to invent some new realm of being to serve as the object of their investigations. Instead they could proceed with their vocation, trying to discover order in collective life. . . . [M]any of them have taken an essentially hermeneutic or if that word frightens, interpretive approach to their task. Interpretive explanation–and it is a form of explanation, not just exalted glossography–trains its attention on what institutions, actions, images, utterances, events, customs, all the usual objects of social sci-

ence interest, mean to those whose institutions, actions, customs, and so on they are.[5]

Interpretive social science is based, most simply, on the observation that life, politics included, is the creation of meanings. Because events in politics, as in the rest of life, never come with their meanings inscribed on them, people expend a great deal of time and effort trying to figure out what events mean. In doing so, they not only interpret the significance of things that just somehow happened; they in a real sense create, by defining, the events themselves. Their assignment of meanings, furthermore, influences what happens next. The bottom line of the interpretive approach, then, is that an act can never be separated from its meaning. To study one requires the study of the other.

The presidency is particularly well suited to the application of the interpretive method. Presidents have, to begin with, been profitably analyzed as "reflectors and carriers of America's political self-understanding."[6] In addition, presidents themselves offer interpretations of what they do. These interpretations were until recently, Tulis notes, treated as "mere epiphenomena" by most political scientists. In fact, they are guides to presidential behavior and on occasion have had powerful political consequences (ibid.). Clearly, presidents both respond to and act upon the public and its ideas about the presidency; neither the president nor the set of culturally embedded expectations with which he interacts is primary. In such a setting, where the dependent and independent variables are constantly trading places, interpretive analysis permits the study of relationships that defy attempts at causal modeling.

HOW AMERICANS THINK ABOUT THEIR PRESIDENT, AND THE DIFFERENCE IT MAKES

The argument I advance in this historical, interpretive book is that we have invested rather *too many* meanings within our presidency. For some presidents, the people's ideas about them are a trap; for others, an instrument of leadership. Whether presidents themselves succeed, however, is not the issue I want to address. For even when presidents manipulate public expectations and thereby "win" politically, as did Ronald Reagan in riding out the storm of Iran-Contra, or Franklin Roosevelt, in asserting prerogative power, they may still fail us.

The real work in establishing this argument gets under way in Chapter One, in which I examine the belief that God has assigned to the American people a special role in the unfolding of His plan for humanity. The idea that the United States represents "the last best hope of earth" is as old as the nation itself, indeed older if this aspect of our self-understanding is acknowledged as a Puritan inheritance.[7] Presidents have relied upon this idea to justify America's entry into war and to provide a rationale for continental expansion. American messianism has even provided a context within which our presidents have sought to call the nation to account for its misdeeds, as in Abraham Lincoln's famous second inaugural address.

America's understanding of itself as a providential nation, and the president's central role in articulating this understanding, have been constants in American history. Through overtly biblical interpretations, presidents have charted the nation's future to the timetable of seals, trumpets, and vials announced by Saint John the Divine. Despite considerable continuity, however, the American civil-religious tradition has proven to be a malleable tool in the hands of our most ambitious heads of state. By incorporating within the civil religion new events, characters, and signs, presidents have moved the nation spiritually, with profound political consequences.

In Chapter Two, I explore the complexities of claims about freedom. In 1775, Dr. Samuel Johnson asked how it could be "that we hear the loudest yelps for liberty among the drivers of negroes."[8] Today, the juxtaposition of freedom and unfreedom in the United States is not as stark. Still, there is no consensus in America about what our national commitment to freedom requires of us. Freedom is an inherently slippery concept, and in America, its ambiguity is magnified by a fixation on the liberties enjoyed by individuals. Communal duties necessarily go along with negative liberties. Freedom *from* one restraint entails the acceptance of freedom *for* another. But America's highly individualistic culture,

I argue, has a blind spot that obscures the interrelatedness of individual and social freedoms. In an examination of the demands for freedom made by and on behalf of African Americans, I show that presidents, as a consequence, have spent more time trying to avoid being caught up in the paradoxes of American ideas about freedom than trying to unravel them.

Chapter Three concerns how Americans think about (or, more precisely, how they try to avoid thinking about) power. To fear power is as American as to demand freedom. Indeed, Americans have been jealous of relinquishing their power over governmental decisions even to their elected representatives. Psychologists tell us that one way to resolve any fear is to dissolve the psychological distance between oneself and the object of one's fear. This, I argue, is the solution Americans have hit upon with respect to the presidency. By appropriating the age-old monarchical conceit that the sovereign is not the agent but the *embodiment* of the nation, Americans have imbued their presidents (at least some of them, some of the time) with charisma. The problem is that "in the search for charisma," as Harvey Mansfield has written, "a democratic people is asking to be fooled, and justifying in advance the levity and irresponsibility of its leaders."[9] Those who lose themselves in support of a charismatic leader hope to participate vicariously in the mysteries of power, without feeling its taint. Through this alchemy of the psyche, the intended presiding officer of the government at times becomes a veritable king, whose pretensions to sovereignty would have dismayed even Alexander Hamilton.

Chapter Four begins with a simple observation: At the same time as we elevate presidents to virtual kingship, we demand that our presidents symbolize our commitment to democracy. America's belief in democracy and its presidential form of government did not merge until Andrew Jackson's presidency. Nevertheless, by 1880, the idea that the nation's chief executive derives his authority from a democratic mandate to translate the majority's will into policy had found its place among the government's hallowed "traditions."[10] Traditions function, of course, to guide and constrain behavior. But in the case of the presidency, the democratic creed has lost much of the utility it once had.

In the nineteenth century, I argue, the creed of democracy and the institution of the presidency fit together better because they were not so often forced together. In the 1800s, that is, democracy was not simply a process that validated the selection of leaders but a substantive goal to be fought for. The term was also used to refer to the popular classes whose interests would most be served if democracy were ever fully realized. Back then, as a consequence, not every president felt compelled to proclaim himself the symbolic carrier of his nation's democratic hopes. Today, democracy is seldom used to refer to a class or to the goal of a domestic political movement. It is a process, and little more. Given the unarguably democratic openness of the contemporary presidential selection process, therefore, every one of our modern presidents, regardless of the character of his agenda or the quality of his character, is by definition an avatar of democracy. As our vocabulary of democracy has lost its range of associations, our ability to distinguish true democrats from democrats of convenience has been stunted. The consequences are demonstrated in a comparison of Andrew Jackson and John F. Kennedy.

In Chapter Five, I further explore the tension revealed in the two preceding chapters between the presidency's democratic legitimacy and its potential as a base for kingly rule. My exploration begins with the observation that the Constitution, perhaps inadvertently, makes the presidency the repository of prerogative powers. Prerogative, in the oft-cited words of John Locke, is the power "to act according to discretion, for the public good, without the prescription of the law, and sometimes even against it."[11] But if prerogative power is not exercised or judged by reference to the laws of our democracy, by what rules does it operate? My answer to this question brings with it good news and bad news.

The good news is that the American public has displayed considerable maturity and common sense in distinguishing between great men ("God-like princes," in Locke's words) and pretenders to that status. The people have granted the former broad latitude, whereas they have rebuffed the claims to prerogative made by the latter. The bad news is that the great men to whom prerogative is granted, though they do not use their power for personal gain, do not always use it wisely. As Locke wrote of the attitudes that English subjects demonstrated toward their kings: "The people are very seldom, or never scrupulous, or nice in the point: they are far from examining prerogative, whilst it is in any tolerable degree imploy'd . . . for the good of the people, and not manifestly against it." In a democracy, this is a very long leash for even a Godlike prince to be on.

But what about a president's more mundane responsibilities: What are his duties and opportunities in normal times, and how can he best do the many jobs that the public and the Constitution assign to him? These down-to-earth concerns are the topic of Chapter Six. A voluminous literature already exists on this aspect of the presidency. (Indeed, the single most influential volume in the field of presidency studies, Richard Neustadt's *Presidential Power*, deals primarily with what might be called presidential craft.)[12] My purpose is not to add to this literature but to critique it, in the context of an analysis of the effect of such volumes and the ideas they contain on the conduct of our presidents.

In Chapter Seven, I propose some less than radical institutional modifications that might help us to get out of the fix that ideas have gotten us into. To begin with, I endorse an argument for the use of proportional representation in elections to the House of Representatives. The result, I argue, could be the harnessing of the presidency to the fortunes of a multiparty coalition in the Congress. The people would be encouraged by such a transformation to think of their president less as a head of state and more as the head of a legislative voting bloc. In tandem with this change, I recommend diffusing the symbolism of national stewardship to embrace other constitutional, and nonconstitutional, figures as well.

SIX IDEAS AT THE HEART OF A DYSFUNCTIONAL RELATIONSHIP

In this book, then, I deal with personalities, institutions, and the ideas of presidents, intellectuals, and the public. I discuss George Washington, Thomas Jefferson, Andrew Jackson, Abraham Lincoln, Woodrow Wilson, Franklin (and Theodore) Roosevelt, Harry Truman, John Kennedy, Lyndon Johnson, Ronald Reagan, George

Bush, and Bill Clinton. Taken together, the chapters of this book provide an introduction to some of the more significant moments in presidential history. But in each chapter, I follow ideas where they lead me. There is, consequently, no single linear sequence from chapter to chapter. And because some presidencies were more eventful than others in shaping our ideas about the office, I return to certain figures more than once: Andrew Jackson, Ronald Reagan, and especially Abraham Lincoln receive more attention than the others. The resulting imbrications remind us that presidents, unlike the author of this book, do not have the luxury of thinking about one symbolic role at a time.

To comment further on how the chapters of this book hang together, we can say that each chapter examines a separate idea at the heart of a dysfunctional relationship. The people relate to their presidents and the presidents to the people in ways that impair the functioning of our polity. The public, in this relationship, is encouraged to be passive but insistent, hopeful yet despairing. As for the president, he is too often either a tragic or a sinister figure. The symbolic associations that surround his office enervate at the same time as they elevate the man in office. If the president is passive and plays the part that has been scripted for him, the people's contradictory and expansive expectations may well overwhelm him. If the president seeks to take charge of the government and to exploit to his own purposes the public's exaggerated hopes and fears, the people may well find themselves being led to destinations they would not have consciously chosen.

What, then, is the picture of the president's relationship with the people which emerges in this book? We are all familiar with persons who are passive yet unreasonably demanding; who have exalted expectations of those in authority but who seek to undermine that authority at every opportunity; who, when excited, may be counted on to pursue a lesser good today rather than a greater one tomorrow. They are our children. When it comes to our relationship with our presidents, we are too often the children.

1

AMERICA, THE REDEEMER

JOHN WILKES BOOTH PULLED THE TRIGGER, BUT IT WAS Satan who conceived the deed for which his mortal accomplice became infamous.[1] Thus it was only fitting that as Abraham Lincoln lay dying, three angels should descend from heaven, ready to crown the martyred president with a wreath of laurel and to point the way heavenward, where the spirit of George Washington awaited to greet his only equal.[2] And when death claimed "the Hero, born of woman," his soul ascended (with Washington as his guide), leaving behind a nation distraught but redeemed.[3] Lincoln's apotheosis, represented at the time in mass-produced engravings and prints, was the logical culmination of a sequence of events similarly infused with deep religious significance by what Lincoln termed this "almost chosen people."[4]

To Walt Whitman, the days and nights of the Civil War seemed filled with "portents," the years themselves "prophetical!"[5] To Julia Ward Howe, the war was a "fiery gospel writ in burnished rows of steel," presaging "the coming of the Lord." To Ralph Waldo Emerson, the war was "an affair of instincts we did not know we had," Lincoln "an instrument of benefit so vast." To Orestes Brownson, a conservative contemporary of Emerson's, the war was the "thunderstorm that purifies the moral and political atmosphere."[6] And to William Henry Furness, an esteemed Unitarian abolitionist, it seemed certain, once Lincoln issued the Emancipation Proclamation, that the war would be the occasion of a "new world" "coming into existence clothed in millennial splendor" (118).

The millennial hope and apocalyptic fear with which Americans responded to Lincoln's death and the war that framed it illustrate the strength of the idea examined in this chapter: that America is a God-favored nation, the "last, best hope of man."[7] Before returning to Lincoln, whose career is central to an understanding of the effect this constellation of ideas has had on the presidency, it is necessary to explore the idea itself and to establish a context within which further analysis of Lincoln's prophecy may proceed.

THE PRESIDENT AND THE CIVIL RELIGION

The American vision of a providential destiny is older than the nation itself. Indeed, more than a century and a half before America declared its independence, and even before the exodus of English Puritans to the colonies, the "idea that God predicted the defeat of evil before the conflagration, and is redeeming that promise" through the agency of a newly chosen people, "began to be taken seriously throughout English-speaking Protestantism."[8] The nationality of the "New Israel" was not settled for the Puritans until after the defeat of Cromwell in England and the subsequent victory, more than a century later, of his heirs in helping to forge the United States of America.[9]

Ironically, given the foundation in the Protestant Reformation of the doctrine of communal election, the civil religion, as it took shape, developed a theory of justification by works. "I always consider the settlement of America with reverence and wonder," John Adams wrote in his diary, "as the opening of a grand scene and design in Providence for the illumination of the ignorant, and the emancipation of the slavish part of mankind all over the earth."[10] America is not only good but good for a purpose. We know, President Bush said in his 1991 State of the Union address, "why the hopes of humanity turn to us. We are Americans; we have a unique responsibility to do the hard work of freedom."[11] In the even more succinct words of President Eisenhower, "America is great because she is good."[12] This belief in an American imperative to do good in the world is at the core of our civil religion.

America, to elaborate the doctrine, is a land of *manifest* destiny. This is so in two ways. First, the nation's fate is to be inscribed in deeds for all to witness, is to be made manifest, in the vanquishing of its enemies and the exultation of its people. Second, America's chosenness is to be confirmed in such acts; the reason for God's having chosen America to do His work is to be apparent, or manifest. America, by virtue of "her superior form of government, her geographical location, her beneficence," deserves to be so chosen.[13] The angst of America, then, is similar to that Max Weber famously analyzed at the individual level among the early American settlers. To maintain confidence in the nation's unique role in the world requires continual demonstrations that when God chose us, He chose well. The stakes involved in such demonstrations are immense. For when appearances seem to contradict America's salvific self-understanding, "dark chaos impends" for the nation's sense of identity and purpose.[14]

That the president should have a central part to play in the drama that flows from these beliefs was perhaps inevitable.[15] The president is the only nationally elected official in the government. The president is also the person designated to preside over the operations of the government, as the man who became our first president presided over the deliberations of the convention that framed the Constitution. The president, consequently, is at the center of the public's consciousness of the state. Even more important, the president, beginning with Washington, has often been at the center of the people's consciousness of themselves as a nation.

In his eight years as president, Washington established precedents that to this day guide American chief executives in the exercise of their duties.[16] Perhaps the most enduring example that Washington set was his performance as head of the American civil religion. Washington did not merely permit the people to venerate his rulership; he actively discharged the responsibilities of a civil-religious leader. Washington called for acts of ritual devotion; he reminded the faithful of the universal stakes attendant upon their devotion to the nation; and in performing these acts he reciprocated the public's reverence for him and thus consecrated the nation as a church.[17]

In his inaugural address, in which Washington dwelled upon the civil-religious theme, the new president proclaimed his dual belief that:

> (1) "No people can be bound to acknowledge and adore the Invisible Hand which conducts the affairs of men more than those of the United States [since] [e]very step by which they have advanced to the character of an independent nation seems to have been distinguished by some token of providential "agency," AND
> (2) "The preservation of the sacred fire of liberty and the destiny of the Republican model of government are justly considered, perhaps, as deeply, as finally, staked on the experiment intrusted to the hands of the American people."[18]

America, Washington was saying in the eloquent, if florid, style of the time, is both a nation fated for glory and a high-stakes gamble, a nation of destiny *and* experiment.[19] A dynamic tension is thus found at the heart of Washington's articulation of the civil religion. As president, each occupant of Washington's office teaches his lesson anew, by carrying on the tradition of civil-religious stewardship in inaugural addresses and in public pronouncements at moments of crisis and celebration. In addition, the most revered of our presidents have wrestled with the lesson's ambiguities and subtly transformed its meanings.

In so doing, presidents have innovated and embellished two different perspectives on civil-religious leadership: one priestly, the other prophetic. In the former mode, the scholar of religion Martin Marty has observed, presidents represent the people before God and in so doing celebrate and comfort the citizenry. Presidents in the latter tradition, by contrast, represent God before the people and call them sternly to judgment.[20] The remainder of this chapter is devoted to an analysis of two presidents in the prophetic tradition, Abraham Lincoln and Woodrow Wilson, and two in the priestly tradition, Andrew Jackson and Ronald Reagan. Our prophetic presidents met with great resistance in their attempts to lead through the performance of this role. The two priestly presidents, by contrast, looked like successes. But even when our priestly presidents exploit the civil religion to the public's satisfaction, they do not thereby serve the nation well. We begin by returning to the subject of this chapter's opening lines, Abraham Lincoln.

TWO PROPHETIC PRESIDENTS

You only have I known of all the families of the earth: therefore I will punish you for all your iniquities.—Amos 3:2

LINCOLN

In a public letter of September 13, 1862, President Lincoln answered his abolitionist critics who, as always, urged him to go further and faster toward emancipation than was his wont. "I hope it will not be irreverent for me to say," Lincoln wrote with classic wit, "that if it is probable that God would reveal his will to others, on a point so connected with my duty, it might be supposed he would reveal it directly to me." "These are not, however," Lincoln continued, "the days of miracles, and I suppose it will be granted that I am not to expect a direct revelation."[21] Such protestations to the contrary notwithstanding, Lincoln did speak prophetically and did so before a nation eager to accept its leader's words as divinely inspired.[22] The stunning thing, though, was what little control Lincoln himself had over the effect and even the interpretation of his prophecy.

President Lincoln's rendering of the war and its meaning reached a climax in his oft-cited second inaugural. Four years before, Lincoln observed in this address, both North and South had dreaded the onset of war. But the nation was divided over slavery, which "all knew . . . was, somehow, the cause of the war." And because one side would "*make* war rather than let the nation survive, and the other would *accept* war rather than let it perish, . . . the war came." When it did, each side "looked for an easier triumph, and a result less fundamental and astounding" than the abolition of the war's cause. But:

> The Almighty has His own purposes. "Woe unto the world because of offences! for it must needs be that offences come; but woe to that man by whom the offence cometh!" If we shall suppose that American slavery is one of those offences which, in the providence of God, must needs come, but which, having continued through His appointed time, He now wills to remove, and that He gives to both North

> and South, this terrible war, as the woe due to those by whom the offence came, shall we discern therein any departure from those divine attributes which the believers in a Living God always ascribe to Him? Fondly do we hope–fervently do we pray–that this mighty scourge of war may speedily pass away. Yet, if God wills that it continue, until all the wealth piled by the bond-men's two hundred and fifty years of unrequited toil shall be sunk, and until every drop of blood drawn with the lash, shall be paid by another drawn with the sword, as was said three thousand years ago, so still it must be said, "the judgments of the Lord, are true and righteous altogether."[23]

Quoting directly from the King James version of Matthew 18:7, Lincoln imputes responsibility for the scourge of the war to North and South alike. That the Christian God might extract a precise measure of suffering from the nation in recompense for its sins Lincoln justifies by a paraphrase of another biblical passage, Psalms 119:137. Lincoln's wording, however, is closer, Ernest Tuveson has commented, to the recollection of this verse in Revelation 16:7, "where a voice from the altar exclaims, after the third angel has poured out his vial, 'Even so, Lord God Almighty, true and righteous *are* thy judgments.'"[24]

What if Lincoln were correct? Lincoln drew the logical inference himself: God would want His people to "finish the work [they] are in; to bind up the nation's wounds" and to do these things "with malice toward none; with charity for all."[25] The war, Lincoln implored his audience to understand, was America's punishment, not its occasion for glory. For the victors (and all were certain by March 1865 who the victors were to be) to mete out additional punishment would be not merely poor policy but blasphemy.

In speaking as he did, the president was attempting a daring task. "Men are not flattered," Lincoln wrote to Thurlow Weed after the address, "to being shown that there has been a difference of purpose between the Almighty and them."[26] Lincoln died, of course, before having to contend with a Congress in whose actions it was difficult to discern any of the spirit of Lincoln on this occasion. Nevertheless, Lincoln's prophecy did not fail completely, or simply.

Lincoln's second inaugural attempted to amend a theme that had been dominant for years in the writings of northern abolitionists. The war, in the eyes of Weed, William Lloyd Garrison, and innumerable northern preachers, was God's judgment upon a guilty nation. But the guilt of the nation, according to most northern interpreters of His will, was not distributed evenly up and down the country. The slave owners of the South were the cause of the conflict, and the war, once emancipation was accepted as a war aim, was a veritable "wreath of glory around our brow."[27] Lincoln himself had contributed to this vision of the war in the issuance of his Emancipation Proclamation on New Year's Day, 1863. The proclamation has been chastised for having "all the moral grandeur of a bill of lading."[28] But in its heyday, it was with justice viewed by the *New York Times* as the most "important and far-reaching document ever issued since the foundation of the government."[29] The Emancipation Proclamation (followed as it was by the Thirteenth Amendment abolishing slavery throughout the United States) had ensured that the war would indeed become what Lincoln in December 1861 had promised it would not: "a violent and remorseless revolutionary struggle."[30]

In the aftermath of assassination, Lincoln was revered by many in the North for his prophetic warnings to slaveholders. He had been slow to come fully to the abolitionist cause, it was widely observed; nevertheless, in the words of Alex Bullock in the eulogy he delivered before the Worcester City Council in 1865, "When you reflect how abnormal and stupendous was the cause he had to manage, I will thank you to tell me if waiting on public opinion was not waiting on Providence itself."[31] But Lincoln's postemancipation urging that the North remain as humble in victory as in the darkest days of the struggle was lost in the aftermath of his death. Following the assassination, "most pulpits thundered that stern justice must be administered upon the South."[32]

Lincoln's second inaugural encompassed popular themes—the evil of slavery and the triumph of freedom in the war. But when it strayed beyond these subjects, his words lost their power. There was, in addition, another reason why Lincoln failed to achieve a full measure of success through his prophecy. The prophet, Lincoln not excepted, is both a prophesier and the fulfillment of earlier prophecies. And it was, and to a considerable extent remains, as the fulfillment of the prophecy of the rise of the West that Lincoln achieved his most durable fame as a symbol of what is sacred to the nation.

The Civil War is erroneously remembered as merely a struggle of North against South; it was also a turning point in the transformation of both regions by their merger with the expanding West. Although he had taken a very public stance against the Democrats' war with Mexico, Lincoln, both as a Whig and a Republican, supported government policies for the settlement, improvement, and expansion of the country. As president, he signed legislation that created the nation's first income tax, license fees on every profession save the ministry, and which turned over millions of acres of land to the railroad companies. In addition, Lincoln signed the famous Morrill Land Grant Act, which laid the foundation for higher education in loyal western states that lacked the collegiate traditions of the East, and the Homestead Act, which opened public lands to settlers in the West.[33] Even Lincoln's struggle to keep the South in the Union was a means to this end of western expansion and settlement. "Proving that popular government is not an absurdity," Lincoln told John Hay shortly after the war commenced, "is the first necessity that is upon us." It was vital to prove democracy sensible, according to Lincoln, because popular government is the guarantor of "an unfettered start, and a fair chance in the race of life." These, Lincoln was certain, were "the leading object of the government for whose existence we contend."[34] Lincoln's words imply that it was to preserve the spirit of American enterprise that slavery had to be kept from spreading westward. The West was the future of America.

In the appropriately religious language of Walt Whitman, writing in 1856:

> As the broad fat States of the West, the largest and best parts of the inheritance of the American farmers and mechanics, were ordained to common people and workmen long in advance by Jefferson, Washington, and the earlier Congresses, now a far ampler West is to be ordained to workmen, or to the masters of workmen? Shall the future mechanics of America be serfs? Shall labor be degraded, and workmen be whipt in the fields for not performing their tasks?

No! Whitman replied. The future of the nation belonged rather to "American young men, a different superior race," and Abraham Lincoln, Whitman came to believe, was the noblest issue of this "superior race."[35] Americans who had learned to see Lincoln in this light may perhaps be forgiven for failing to appreciate fully his later statements on the meaning of the war.[36]

Unintentionally ironic testimony to the power of this aspect of the Lincoln symbol was given in 1865 by Ralph Waldo Emerson in his eulogy for the slain president. Lincoln's life was indeed evidence of God's concern for an anxious race. But the race at the center of the Civil War was not African-born. Rather, it was the "race" of the American common (and nonsouthern) person. At first, Emerson observed, the eastern states were disappointed with Lincoln. But then they came to appreciate the "profound good opinion which the people of Illinois and of the West had conceived of him." Emerging from his "middle-class" background to lead "this middle-class country," Lincoln was "the true history of the American people in his time. Step by step he walked before them." And that history and the man who embodied it proved, Emerson concluded, that "there is a serene Providence which rules the fate of nations." It cares little for any single generation or any one battle, but it works toward a great purpose:

> the ultimate triumph of the best race by the sacrifice of everything which resists the moral laws of the world. It makes its own instruments, creates the man for the time, trains him in poverty, inspires his genius, and arms him for his task. It has given every race its own talent, and ordains that only that race which combines perfectly with the virtues of all shall endure.[37]

Lincoln the frontiersman, the "Prince of Rails," "honest Abe," the teller of tall tales, was the Lincoln revered on this and a great many other occasions.[38]

Lincoln himself expressed best the relationship of the two aspects of his prophetic appeal: "In *giving* freedom to the *slave*, we *assure* freedom to the *free*–honorable alike in what we give, and what we preserve. We shall nobly save, or meanly lose, the last best hope of earth."[39] To save the Union so that the nation could realize its promise was paramount. To do so while at the same time emancipating slaves added nobility to the enterprise.

WILSON

While Lincoln thought he had discovered the greater meaning of the Civil War, Woodrow Wilson knew differently. Speaking to Confederate veterans two months after his address to Congress asking for a declaration of war against Germany, Wilson prophesied—explaining the ways of God. Veterans of the Confederacy, Wilson began, have not been alone in "wonder[ing] at some of the dealings of Providence." But the plan of the Almighty, "which we were incapable of conceiving" at the time, reveals now its "definiteness of purpose":

> And now that we see ourselves part of a nation united, powerful, great in spirit and in purpose, we know the great ends which God, in His mysterious providence, wrought through our instrumentality, because at the heart of the men of the North and of the South there was the same love of self-government and of liberty, and now we are to be an instrument in the hands of God to see that liberty is made secure for mankind.[40]

The purpose of the Civil War, Wilson was saying, was to strengthen the common bonds of the American people so as to prepare them for the world war into which Wilson had reluctantly (albeit with sublime expectations) led them.

We think less of the First World War for having experienced the Second. But at the time, it was not only Wilson who saw in it "the supreme test of the nation."[41] Wilson's understanding of that test was, however, extreme. The president firmly believed that the war was a "war to end all wars" and that in winning this war, as Wilson, when it was over, asserted his troops had done, Americans had fulfilled the promise that God made to the world when He secured America's independence. In the War for Independence, Americans had but "served [them]selves." In the world war, Americans met with the opportunity to "serve mankind," "not only to defend [their] own rights as a nation but to defend also the rights of free men throughout the world."[42]

In the war's aftermath, Wilson asserted time and again that America had worked an act of redemption. When the people of Europe first saw "that gallant emblem of the stars and stripes upon their fields," they thought it was only moral encouragement that

the U.S. troops would offer them. Soon, they realized the magnitude of the American commitment. In the end, Wilson proclaimed in Cheyenne, Wyoming, on September 24, 1919, "America had the infinite privilege of fulfilling her destiny and saving the world."[43] But the struggle was not over. America had won the war; now Wilson thought he must win the peace. The United States, Wilson told another audience in the summer of 1919, "said to mankind at her birth: 'We have come to redeem the world by giving it liberty and justice.' Now we are called upon . . . to redeem that immortal pledge."[44]

To walk away from this opportunity, Wilson was certain, would provoke the wrath of God. In a poetic interlude in another speech from his western tour, Wilson spoke of the consequences should his plan for the peace, the League of Nations, not be acknowledged as the "conscience of the world." "There will come sometime, in the vengeful Providence of God," Wilson foretold, "another struggle in which, not a few hundred thousand fine men from America will have to die, but as many millions as are necessary to accomplish the final freedom of the people of the world."[45] It was, thus, with tremendous self-assurance that he had seen the right and that the stakes were enormous, that Wilson sought to represent the intentions of God to the people of "His" country.

Wilson's faith in his ability to perceive the design of the Lord's plan for America was complemented by a similarly unshakable faith in his ability, as a great leader, to "interpret" the public mood and thus lead the people to a vantage point from which they, too, would see the truth and act according to its self-evident imperatives.[46] The leader, Wilson once explained, is an "interpreter" of the "common thought." The voice of the leader must "ring with the voice of the people." He cannot speak airily or abstractly, or even pedagogically, for "men are not led by being told what they don't know" but by having revealed some truth that is latent within them.[47] The leader must work, in other words, with the human material at hand.

Despite its reliance on the people as they are, the leader's task as Wilson conceived it is utterly alien to what is today called "following the polls." It is, rather, like the artistry of a sculptor:

> He [the leader] supplies the power; others supply only the materials upon which that power operates. The power will fail if it be misapplied; it will be misapplied if it be not suitable both in its character and in its method to the nature of the materials upon which it is spent; but that nature is, after all, only its means. It is the power which dictates, dominates; the materials yield. (25–26)

By supplying the force of his own "power" to the raw "materials" that are his audience, the consummate leader molds people as an artist molds clay. The leader, like the sculptor committed to that simple medium, cannot substitute for clay some more elegant or refined substance.[48] But if it is given to him "to hear the inarticulate voices that stir in the night-watches, apprising the lonely sentinel of what the day will bring forth," he may make of the raw stuff of the people a force for some great purpose–even the saving of the world.[49] Great leaders, by speaking large, elemental truths to the people, "compel obedience." "Men know they speak justice, and obey by instinct" (54). Or as Wilson said during the first of his western tour speeches in 1919: "Some gentlemen have feared with regard to the League of Nations that we will be obliged to do things we do not want to do. If the treaty were wrong, that might be so, but if the treaty is right, we will wish to preserve right." Wilson was confident that the league would never be at variance with American opinion because he was confident that he knew "the heart of this great people."[50]

President Wilson had read, or so he thought, the "Spirit of the Age."[51] He knew also, or so he believed, "the real spirit of the American people."[52] And in 1919, "this interesting year of grace" as Wilson called it, it was God's intention that the two spirits merge. On that day of communion, Wilson prophesied, "all this debate will seem in our recollection like a strange mist that came over the minds of men here and there in the Nation," and the world will know "that of a sudden, upon the assertion of the real spirit of the American people, they came to the edge of the mist, and outside lay the sunny country where every question of duty lay plain and clear and where the great tramp, tramp of the American people sounded in the ears of the whole world, which knew that the armies of God were on their way."[53]

Wilson's effort to win American inclusion in the League of Nations covenant, to claim for the nation its destiny, was a failure. Too many commentators have interpreted this failure with the Book of Numbers as their model: The people failed their prophet.[54] Perhaps we should be bold enough to insist rather that the prophet failed his people. Indeed, with the experience of Lincoln also in mind, it should be said that presidents might do well to avoid prophecy altogether. To believe otherwise is to risk elevating the hold that those prophets' anguished lives and deaths have on our imaginations over the more mundane task of evaluating the efficacy of prophecy as an instrument of leadership.

TWO PRIESTLY PRESIDENTS

Ye are the light of the world. A City that is set on an hill cannot be hid.—Matt. 5:14

JACKSON

The person responsible for discovering the practical potential of the president's priestly role, whereby the president represents the people before God, was Andrew Jackson. Drawing upon the civil religion's implicit doctrine of justification by works, Jackson exhorted the people to demonstrate their chosenness by supporting his leadership. In the process, Jackson amended the nation's spiritual narrative, assigning for the first time a salvific role to the contemporaneous electoral majority.

Jackson was first elected to the presidency in 1828, in one of the most intensely personal and shameful elections in American history. During the campaign the supporters of the leading contenders traded bitter barbs, and the winner's side harped incessantly on the charge of a "corrupt bargain" that allegedly had given the office four years in the past to the incumbent, John Quincy Adams. To Jackson's supporters, "Old Hickory" was not, then, the champion of a program in 1828 but the reflection of the people. Like the plain people of America, his supporters boasted, Andrew Jackson had been "never to Europe," "never the head of a department," and never, for that matter, to college.[55] When Jackson, who had won the popular vote in 1824, was denied the election, the people, Jackson's supporters proclaimed for the next four years, were cheated. The very freedom of the country was at stake in avenging this perfidy. Jackson's opponents were bemused. Thus, in the aftermath of the 1828 campaign, a perplexed Daniel Webster remarked that people came from five hundred miles away to see their champion (Jackson) and that they "really seem[ed] to think that the country [had] been rescued from some dreadful danger."[56]

In Jackson's successful bid for reelection in 1832, he brought out to the fullest the sacerdotal implications of his leadership. The center of attention in this, his second successful presidential campaign, was Jackson's declared "war" against the Second Bank of the United States, the "Monster Bank" whose rechartering was favored by his opponents. At stake in this contest, Jackson suggested, was the success or failure of the entire God-granted American mission in popular government.

The question, Jackson declared in his fifth annual message to Congress, was "whether the people of the United States [were] to govern through representatives chosen by their unbiased suffrages or whether the money and power of a great corporation [were] to be secretly exerted to influence their judgment and control their decisions."[57] Jackson might, he stated in reply to the Senate's censure of his removal of government funds from the bank, have "sold [him]self to its designs." But the motive force that led him, the president stated, would not permit such an act. For the president was driven by "an anxious desire and a fixed determination to return to the people unimpaired the sacred trust they ha[d] confided to [his] charge."[58] The sacred trust of the people in their president, moreover, was the mirror image to Jackson of another confidence. "You have the highest of human trusts committed to your care," Jackson reminded the people in his farewell address. "Providence has showered on this favored land blessings without number, and has chosen you as the guardians of freedom, to preserve it for the benefit of the human race."[59]

This view of the president as a delegate, charged by an electoral majority with a sacred trust to keep the nation on course toward its destiny, represented a substantial innovation in the presidential interpretation of the people's and the president's roles in the civil religion. Washington, for a notable contrary example, had spoken in his farewell address of the sanctity of the *limits* to popular sovereignty. Although, Washington observed, "the basis of our political system is the right of the people to make and to alter their constitutions of government," "the constitution which at any time exists till changed by the explicit and authentic act of the whole people is sacredly obligatory upon all."[60] As for the public and their relation to the president, Washington had suggested in his first inaugural the limited relevance of their wishes or votes to the actions he intended to take in office. In that speech's most concrete reference to a matter of policy (the Bill of Rights), Washington made plain his conviction that presidents are not to be directed by the people. Because, Washington stated, he "could be guided by no lights derived from official opportunities" in offering his recommendation on the subject, he would leave the matter to the members of the legislature to decide.[61]

To depart from this principle would apparently be to inflame the "spirit of party" and thus risk the "ruins of public liberty."[62] Because, as we observed above, Washington held the fate of liberty in the entire world to be at stake in the American experiment, such an outcome would be a religious catastrophe. Jackson's other predecessors expressed similar views. All agreed that for America to attain its destiny, the people must maintain public virtue; but this was commonly interpreted as a proscription against rather than a prescription for the contemporaneous demonstration of the people's will.[63]

REAGAN

The editors of the *New Republic* were precisely wrong about Ronald Reagan. "We elected a President, not a priest," they insisted in an editorial excoriating Reagan for his religiously suffused leadership.[64] That it fell to Reagan, as president, to exercise priestly responsibilities is not remarkable. Reagan's political use of this role, however, was exceptional, in ways recalling Andrew Jackson. Echoing his distant predecessor, Reagan spoke often of his cause as a spiritual mission. Reagan even asked for a moment of prayer to consecrate "our crusade" at the close of his speech accepting the Republican nomination in 1980. Just before this point in his address, the candidate had asked a telling question: "Can we doubt," he said, "that only a Divine Providence [could have] placed this land, this island of freedom, here as a refuge for all those people in the world who yearn to breathe freely?"[65]

Ironically, Reagan's rhetorical question was powerful because, when he asked it, more Americans than before *were* doubting the millennial vision of their country.[66] In a reflection of such doubts, Jimmy Carter had spoken in that same year, as he had often in the past, of the limits circumscribing American power and, even, American righteousness. "We've learned the uses and the limitations of power," Carter confessed. But there is power enough, he implied, to fulfill a dream. "I want from the bottom of my heart," the outgoing president continued, "to remove the blight of racial and other discrimination from the face of our nation."[67]

Carter did not differ from Reagan in believing that the key to America's strength lay in America's faith. The difference was that Carter's rhetoric, replete as it was with the imagery of "blight," seemed to cast doubt upon that faith's resolve. Well before his infamous "malaise" speech of the summer of 1979, in which the president seemed to blame the American people's lack of faith for his presidency's failures, Carter, in his inaugural address, suggested that America's spiritual core had weakened. "His overwhelming concern," Samuel Beer observed, quoting from Carter's inaugural, "was with 'a *new* national spirit of unity and trust.'" And although a president, Carter intoned, "may sense and proclaim" such a new force, "only a people can provide it." Carter seemed unable in this most important of his public speeches to locate that which he promised to rely upon.[68]

Reagan's America is also a land of faith. But Reagan's rhetoric takes for granted what Carter searched for. "If faith is the essential American virtue for Reagan, skepticism and pessimism are un-American vices. The believing heart is threatened by the doubting head," writes Bruce Miroff.[69] "Can we solve the problems confronting us?" Reagan asked in his first inaugural. "The answer is an unequivocal and emphatic 'yes.'" And why? Because as "this breed called Americans," "we have every right to dream heroic dreams." And what is at stake? Again, the God-granted destiny of the American experiment in popular government. "When they arrived at Plymouth, Massachusetts," Reagan said in his acceptance speech, "they formed what they called a 'compact.'" That act, Reagan professed, "set the pattern for what was to come." In 1980, Reagan continued, it was "once again time to renew our compact," "for the sake of this, our beloved and blessed land."

Slightly misquoting the spiritual leader of theocratic New England, Reagan similarly and insistently stated his belief that America was a "shining city upon a hill."[70] To John Winthrop, the original governor of the Massachusetts Bay Colony, the new land's topographical location was a promise but also a warning, and the city did not shine:

> We shall be as a city upon a hill, the eyes of all people are upon us; so that if we shall deal falsely with our God in this work we have undertaken and so cause Him to withdraw his present help from us, we shall be made a story and a by-word through the world. We shall open the mouths of enemies to speak evil of the ways of God and all professions for God's sake. We shall shame the faces of many of God's worthy servants and cause their prayers to be turned into curses upon us till we be consumed out of the good land wither we are going.[71]

The Massachusetts Puritans had work to do to make their good land shine. In Reagan's use of the metaphor, the glow, like the goodness from which it emanates, is assumed. All the American people have to do is believe in themselves. The "crisis" facing America, Reagan stated at his inauguration, does not require the sacrifices of a soldier on the field of battle. It requires merely "our best effort and our willingness to believe in ourselves and to believe in our capacity to perform great deeds."[72]

Reagan's celebratory employment of civil-religious themes was more passive than Jackson's. In part, this reflected different political circumstances. In the 1980s, there was no demon bank to be subdued, no Senate censure to condemn, no party to build from scratch. But this does not mean that Reagan's priestly rhetoric was of no practical consequence. Historians and political scientists will long debate whether the 1980s were as significant to the course of the nation as Reagan held them to be. But few doubt that Reagan's fiscal policies, military buildup, and assertion of personality powerfully shaped the politics as well as the public discourse of his time in a way not seen since the 1930s. And without Reagan's employment of civil-religious themes on the campaign trail as well as in office, it is doubtful that he would have had such an impact on the government and the nation. Truly, in Reagan's administration "civil religion reached a new pinnacle in the American experience as it was exalted by a powerful, priestly President."[73]

CONCLUSION

Each president is head of the American civil religion. Each president is therefore given a tool for leadership which no senator, governor, or member of the House of Representatives can lay claim to. When calling the people to join him in advancing the sacred cause of American nationhood, a president reaches deep into the collective psyche of the nation. For more than two hundred years, Americans have heard such claims. Often, they have responded as the president wished; at other times, they have turned a deaf ear to his prayers.

The president must be careful in exercising civil-religious leadership. Of the presidents discussed in this chapter, two attempted to lead the people by interpreting for them God's will. These presidents stood before their people as did Moses. Moses, it bears remembering, once angered God. As punishment, God permitted him to see, but not to enter, the Promised Land. This brings to mind a question. If God does exist, and He does take an interest in this nation, what is the probability that an American president's attempts at prophecy will be any better rewarded than were Moses'? Like many questions worth pondering, this one is utterly unanswerable.

We are not, however, without answers to some more worldly questions along the same lines. Prophetic leadership was costly for President Lincoln and, especially, President Wilson. We will never know, of course, whether President Lincoln would have repeated the effort he made in his second inaugural to humble the victors and, if he had, whether he would have won northern Republicans to the cause of a nonmalicious Reconstruction. Certainly his successor had no luck along these lines. A more complete test of the prophetic style of leadership was made by President Wilson.

It may sound harsh, but it is nevertheless true that while Wilson prophesied, the nation burned. As the president concentrated on his civil-religious mission, domestic troubles multiplied. In the vacuum of presidential leadership, Attorney General A. Mitchell Palmer began his infamous raids against alleged subversives, and race riots occurred in major northern cities. There were, in addition, railroad strikes, a national steel strike, and a police strike in Boston.[74] Even Wilson's stroke of October 2, 1919, suffered while he was on his western tour, cannot explain the president's seeming abdication of responsibility to help shape the government's response to such worldly, but momentous, events.

The consequences of priestly leadership are similarly troubling. Priestly presidents, to begin with, encourage voters to make the same mistake that the prophetic Woodrow Wilson invited them to make: to overlook mundane realities, substituting for them fantastical crusades. The people rebuffed Wilson, so we shall never know what difficulties, if any, would have flowed from the implementation of Wilson's plans for the peace. In the case of our two priestly presidents, though, the public accepted the president's interpretation of reality and paid the price. Economic recession followed Jackson's war against the evil bank. The federal government was also fated by Jackson's success to undergo industrialization without the potential benefits of national monetary controls. Reagan's 1981 legislative victories were followed by historically unique levels of peacetime public debt. Overall government indebtedness in 1993 was in fact higher than "at any other time since the mid-1950s, when we were still paying off the costs of the Second World War."[75] Some supply-side economists insist that this flood of red ink has nothing to do with the policies of the Reagan administration.[76] What seems less contestable is that the memory of Reagan's feel-good leadership makes dealing with the deficit (and a host of other issues) tremendously difficult.

The problems inherent in the civil-religious presidency are poignantly brought home in the difficulties that successors to crusading presidents face when they attempt to bring the nation's attention back to earth. Even if we leave aside the well-known failures of these crusaders' immediate successors—Martin Van Buren, Andrew Johnson, Warren Harding, and George Bush—we can find ample evidence that crusaders in the White House leave troublesome legacies for those who follow them.

Consider William Henry Harrison's victory of 1840. The Whig successor to the Jacksonians electioneered like a Democrat. In fact, his log cabin and hard-cider campaign excited a surge to the polls which exceeded the turnout for either of Jackson's victories. But to win, Harrison had to make himself party to a lie: that he was a simple frontiersman, not much different (and certainly no better than!) Old Hickory himself. (In truth, Harrison, born in Virginia, was the son of a wealthy plantation owner.) Harrison's anticlimactic inaugural address, in which he spoke in his true, dignified, and boring voice, included a lecture on the executive's role in government which Harrison's campaign had plainly contradicted. And let us not overlook the situation of Bill Clinton. When he came to office, he found himself impaled on the horns of the same dilemma that had made George Bush's domestic presidency so frustrating. If Clinton were to address the policy legacies of the Reagan administration, and in particular the government's burden of debt, he faced two possibilities. His first option was to appropriate the myth of America's chosenness as the justification for repudiating commitments that Reagan had made. (This we might call the "Reagan got God wrong" strategy.) This is one way to read what Clinton was up to in the rhetorical emphasis he placed in his acceptance speech on the theme of a "New Covenant."[77] But civil-religious leadership is a little like pulling a rabbit out of a hat. Anyone can say the magic words; not everyone gets the rabbit. The failure in 1993 of Clinton's rhetoric to win for him the sort of mass support which Reagan enjoyed left him with a second option. He had somehow to repudiate Reagan's policies without seeming to reject Reagan's powerful articulation of the American civil-religious story. (This is the "You've got Reagan wrong" approach.) It should not surprise us if Clinton does not find an easy path out of this forest.

The people and their presidents are united by bonds whose intensity and range are moving. If we were to judge politics purely by the standards of drama, the presidents for whom civil religion was most valuable would rate high marks. But if we are to demand more of our politics, and our politicians, we have already uncovered some grounds for concern. Though we have only begun our analysis, the presidency is not off to a good start.

2

IT'S A FREE COUNTRY

"IT'S A FREE COUNTRY!" "FREEDOM NOW!" IF THE FORmer, why the latter? If America is the home of the free, why is our political history punctuated by demands for that which we already possess in alleged abundance? One answer, favored by old-time civics texts and two centuries of presidential rhetoric, is contained in the fairy-tale version of America's history and prospects: In this God-favored land, people first found the courage to rest government upon the judgment of individuals free to think, speak, and write what they pleased. But not every American at first enjoyed the liberties promised, implicitly, to all. As time passed, the tale continues, freedom was spread throughout the land, embracing those who were at first excluded. In time, America will bring freedom to all the peoples of the world.

In this naive narrative, presidents are assigned pivotal roles. Andrew Jackson won the economic emancipation of working people. Abraham Lincoln freed the slaves and "remade America" in the process.[1] Woodrow Wilson, the educator-as-president, helped teach freedom to the world. Lyndon Johnson was seemingly two men. The bad Johnson sent American soldiers to die in a futile, if not immoral, war in Vietnam; the good Johnson granted African Americans the freedom to vote. There is a measure of truth to these statements; such is the nature of myth. But these assertions, and the fairy tale that they embellish, grossly misrepresent the dynamics of the contest over freedom in American politics and the president's involvement in that struggle.

To some, freedom means the right to abortion on demand, to others the right of fetal maturation. Prohibitionists thought they were emancipating a nation in bondage to the demon of alcohol. Before the Civil War, some Americans believed that the abolition of slavery was the very least that freedom demanded; to others abolition threatened the freedom of the owners of slaves. The slipperiness of the concept reveals its roots. In every instance, freedom is the realization of what the speaker holds to be the authentic nature of his or her, or some other person's, self.

In the words of the philosopher Frithjof Bergman, "an act is free if the agent identifies with the elements from which it flows." Freedom, therefore, "is not a primary but a derivative notion," dependent as it is on one's understanding of what it means to be a person.[2] Whatever inauthentically constrains a man or woman, whatever prevents a person from *being* a person, negates freedom. With so many conflicting ideas about personhood–Is the slave a person? was a much-contested question a mere 130 years ago; today the status of human zygotes is debated with similar intensity–it is difficult to forge consensus on the boundaries of freedom. The libertarian solution, "you do your thing, and I'll do mine," will not work when what one side wants is to make slaves (literally or metaphorically) of the other. "The shepherd," as Lincoln said in 1864, "drives the wolf from the sheep's throat, for which the sheep thanks the shepherd as a *liberator*, while the wolf denounces him for the same act as the destroyer of liberty."[3]

And what of the shepherd: Is he too free? To answer this question, an American would likely want to know: Did the shepherd choose his own vocation? Is he happy being a shepherd? Did saving the sheep provide him with emotional or spiritual gratification? In America's predominantly individualistic culture, to be a person means to be in control of one's life. The authentic self would seem to be pure will, stripped of all involuntary associations and responsibilities.[4] Consequently, we value dearly freedom from constraints, what Isaiah Berlin famously characterized as negative liberty. Positive liberty, the freedom to be not "your own person" but a member of some community–with rules that circumscribe the individual's behavior–is a notion that many Americans have difficulty comprehending, much less embracing.[5]

Since we all believe in freedom but cannot always agree on its definition–whether for the sheep, the wolf, or the shepherd–we witness a constant struggle for power among groups in conflict over freedom's meaning. And because the American government, whose powers of coercion and persuasion are coveted by those engaged in such contests, is so famously separated, checked, balanced, and otherwise fragmented, the struggle to define freedom typically takes the form of a turf war: an effort to achieve a preponderance of power within one of the institutions of government.

The president, of course, occupies some of the most coveted turf in the political universe. But it is turf that does not allow its possessors to acknowledge openly this aspect of its character. Our presidents, from Washington on, have sought to portray themselves—even, or especially, in the heat of partisan battle—as the embodiment of the whole nation. Not only is this good politics, it is incumbent as a consequence of the president's symbolic role as leader of the faithful. Unfortunately for our presidents, then, crusades for freedom more often than not threaten to polarize and tear apart the nation they strive to unite. Nevertheless, and despite the risks, presidents have on occasion found it expedient to enter into conflicts over freedom.

The consequence, explored in the remainder of this chapter, has been a recurring pattern of caution bordering on indifference punctuated by bursts of presidential activism. Presidential activism on behalf of freedom is itself predictably followed by new demands for new conceptions of freedom. This pattern is traced below in the record of the Lincoln, Truman, and Kennedy/Johnson administrations, with regard to the most enduring problematic of American freedom: the political status of African Americans.

LINCOLN

Abraham Lincoln abhorred slavery. "As an adult," J. David Greenstone has noted, "he wrote to an old friend that he hated 'to see the poor creatures hunted down.'" Slaveholders must appreciate "how much the great body of Northern people do crucify their feelings [out of] loyalty to the Constitution and the Union."[6] Lincoln was no abolitionist, and he was certain that the authors of the Declaration of Independence had not intended "to declare all men equal *in all respects.*"[7] Still, who could deny, he wondered, that the Negro is a person and as such is the "equal of every living man" "in the right to eat the bread, without leave of anybody else, which his own hand earns."[8] Even more than he despised slavery, however, Lincoln was devoted to the Union. And, paradoxically, Lincoln loved his country, as he said of his adult political hero, Henry Clay, "partly because it was his own country, but mostly because it was a free country."[9]

As president, Lincoln struggled to unravel the tension between these positions. At first, he thought he could do so peacefully. Indeed, Lincoln, like Clay, longed to be a conciliator. If those on the extreme ends of public opinion, the secessionists and the abolitionists, would but listen to the "better angels of [their] nature," Lincoln averred at the close of his first inaugural address, war could be avoided. And if war were avoided, the Union would be preserved and the western territories reserved for free white settlers eager to partake of the American dream. As for slavery, it could be tolerated until it expired, gradually and without the shedding of white men's blood.[10] As it happened, of course, Lincoln decided he could not countenance the avoidance of war, and in the war he worked out for himself and the nation some new answers, and questions, to the riddle of freedom.

For the first year and a half of war, President Lincoln, anxious about the loyalty of the border states, worked to restrain abolitionist sentiment. (As the president explained on one occasion, he would have liked to have had God on his side, but he had to have Kentucky.)[11] This of course angered the abolitionists, who would gladly have sacrificed the Constitution, and even the Union, to cleanse the nation of the sin of slavery. Indeed, before the war, some abolitionists, most prominently William Lloyd Garrison, favored the secession of slave states. Slaves were to be sacrificed for the cause of eliminating (from within national borders) slavery![12]

Lincoln most plainly expressed his position on the interrelatedness of freedom for the slaves and the freedom guaranteed by the Constitution in a public letter to Horace Greeley. "If I could save the Union," Lincoln wrote in the summer of 1862, "without freeing any slave I would do it, and if I could save it by freeing all the slaves I would do it; and if I could save it by freeing some and leaving others alone, I would also do that." This, Lincoln stated in conclusion, was his view of "official duty." He meant, however, "no modification of [his] oft-expressed personal wish that all men everywhere could be free."[13] The Union, Lincoln here reiterated, was the highest cause to be defended in the war.

To issue an executive proclamation freeing slaves would threaten this war aim, Lincoln explained on numerous occasions in the same year. After all, Lincoln asked, "What good would a proclamation from me do? . . . I do not want to issue a document that the whole world will see must necessarily be inoperative, like the Pope's bull against the comet!"[14] Lincoln was further constrained by his long-held Whig interpretation of the president's role within the government. He had, in fact, earlier in the year vetoed on constitutional grounds an act of Congress providing for the liberation of slaves "confiscated" in the war. "[W]e may not touch property," he proclaimed in his veto message.[15] There was, in addition, the nagging issue of the border states to be considered. And finally, as Lincoln was at pains to explain to a group lobbying for immediate emancipation, there was the fact that the nation already had "an important principle to rally and unite the people." "Constitutional government" was at stake, "a fundamental idea," Lincoln said, "going down about as deep as any thing."[16]

For all these reasons, Lincoln proceeded with caution until what had been threatening became expedient. This happened on September 22, 1862, when the president issued the initial Emancipation Proclamation. The initial proclamation was a threat to the rebellious states: Surrender arms or your slaves shall be proclaimed free. There was, of course, no immediate effect on any slave. Even when the president made good on this threat in his final Emancipation Proclamation, signed on New Year's Day, 1863, no slave was immediately freed as a consequence.[17] Still, the proclamations were momentous, for they set the government on an abolitionist course from which it did not veer. New Year's Day, 1863, was, Ralph Waldo Emerson wrote in the *Atlantic Monthly*, "a day which most . . . dared not hope to see."[18]

Had Lincoln changed? Had he converted to the cause of abolitionism? Was this not indeed the act of a saint, of Father Abraham, a man who would risk all to do what was right?

Not really. Emancipation, to begin with, was a military boon to the North, as freed slaves were conscripted in the tens of thousands into Union ranks. The freedmen fought in major battles, and their valor demoralized the South. Second, the proclamations were limited to territories in rebellion. The border states, which had rejected Lincoln's pleas for voluntary emancipation, were to remain "free" to choose slavery, at least for the time being. Emancipation, in short, helped the North win the war.

It was expedient, furthermore, in a deeper sense, for it permitted Lincoln an extraordinary opportunity for which he longed. In saving the Union he redefined the nation.[19] The United States, Lincoln had long held, was founded upon "a proposition, which had hitherto been considered, at least no better, than problematical; namely, *the capability of a people to govern themselves.*"[20] In a special message to Congress, delivered after shots had been fired at Fort Sumter, Lincoln elaborated on this conviction. The Civil War, Lincoln said, presented to the world the issue of whether "a democracy–a government of the people, by the same people" could survive.[21] Lincoln's turn toward abolition allowed him to merge this faith in America as imbued with a sacred trust to prove the effectiveness of popular government with another conviction, an "ancient faith." "If the Negro is a man," Lincoln once remarked before becoming president, "why then my ancient faith teaches me that 'all men are created equal'; and that there can be no moral right in connection with one man's making a slave of another."[22]

Lincoln's new synthesis was revealed in the first paragraph of the Gettysburg Address:

> Four score and seven years ago our fathers brought forth, upon this continent, a new nation, conceived in liberty, and dedicated to the proposition that "all men are created equal."

The constitutional Union had been founded three score and sixteen years in the past. Lincoln's dating directs us not to that founding but to the earlier Revolution and its Declaration of Independence.

As for the present:

> Now we are engaged in a great civil war, testing whether that nation, or any nation so conceived and so dedicated, can long endure.

The war was an experiment: Can a nation founded upon equality as a "proposition" survive? The "truth" of equality, in Lincoln's rendering, was not self-evident, as it was in the words of Thomas Jefferson. The proposition was, in fact, blatantly false to a large portion of the population and had been since the words were first written. The war was to determine not the truth of the proposition–that was either evident, as it was to the abolitionists, or it was not. Rather, the war was to test the limits of a coercion made necessary by the very fact that this "self-evident" truth was nothing of the sort.

> It is rather for us to be here dedicated to the great task remaining before us–that from these honored dead we take increased devotion to that cause for which they gave the last full measure of devotion–that we here highly resolve that these dead shall not have died in vain–that this nation, under God, shall have a new birth of life–and that government of the people, by the people, for the people, shall not perish from the earth.[23]

Here Lincoln reintroduces his older theme, of the war as a trial of popular government. But the theme has changed. The nation will have, as a result of the war, not simply a restoration of the status quo ante but a "new birth." The nation will experience a new freedom from enslavement, as well as a newly secured freedom of the laws. These two freedoms–one negative, releasing slaves from bondage, and one positive, binding a people (slaves included, if peripherally) together–were Lincoln's twin war aims from 1863 on.

As Civil War historian James McPherson has written, "The United States went to war in 1861 to preserve the *Union*; it emerged from war in 1865 having created a *nation*."[24] The nation was characterized by the synthesis of Lincoln's, and the American people's, two views of freedom. On the one hand, the nation, like the Union, was a government of laws. Lawful government was antithetical to secessionist anarchy and the sort of mob violence caused by abolitionists as well as their opponents before the war. On the other hand, there was the tangible freedom brought about by the destruction of human slavery.

Lincoln sought to teach that negative and positive liberty are intertwined: that freedom means freedom from evil constraints, not the nonsensical freedom from all restraints. As in Chapter One's account of Lincoln's attempt at prophetic leadership, so this story ends also with tragedy. The president's view was a minority opinion, and it was not embraced by the people who began to revere Lincoln once he was (safely) in his grave. Positive freedom, to reiterate, is the right to live according to the laws, without embarrassment or hypocrisy. With respect to freed slaves, positive liberty would have required that they be permitted to live lawfully among their former masters; to compete equally with white men for jobs and homes; to be the masters of their own fate. This, of course, did not happen. Even Lincoln was ambivalent about the extent to which the positive liberty won in the war was to be extended to blacks. The nation had been reconsecrated to lawful union through the North's victory, and the white people of both sections could now get back to the conquest of the West. But could blacks and whites be bound together as well?

President Lincoln apparently could not bring himself to hope so. Even after he issued the initial Emancipation Proclamation, Lincoln continued, as he had for many years, to advocate the voluntary resettlement of freed blacks in either Africa or Central America.[25] Lincoln was, in his words, "horrified at the thought" of miscegenation and even defended the Republican party's antislavery policy on the grounds that slavery, which tolerated the rape of black slaves by their white masters, had been responsible by 1850 for the birth of 405,751 mulattoes in the United States. Freed blacks and free whites, Lincoln believed, should not and would not "mix."[26]

To Lincoln, racial antipathy was the converse of race pride, of which he approved. Thus, in seeking to persuade a committee of free blacks in August 1862 to take up the government's offer to help them resettle outside the United States, Lincoln held up the example of the "father of his country," George Washington. The free blacks to whom he spoke, Lincoln knew, would suffer personal hardship in leaving their country. Nevertheless, they should go, in emulation of "General Washington," who "himself endured greater physical hardships than if he had remained a British subject" yet was "a happy man, because he was engaged in benefiting his race."[27] Lincoln's words, and the hundreds of thousands of dollars appropriated to promote resettlement, were to no avail. Men and women of African descent remained for the most part in the United States, a "troublesome presence" and a continual "embarrassment" to Lincoln.[28]

The story hardly ends there, however. For embarrassment is one of the more underrated of political motives. It spurred Lincoln toward the abolitionist stance. "I hate it," he said once, in 1854, of slavery, "because it deprives our republican example of its just influence in the world–enables the enemies of free institutions, with plausibility, to taint us as hypocrites."[29] And just over eighty years after Lincoln's death, embarrassment spurred another midwestern president–who shared fully in the pride of race which Abraham Lincoln took for granted–to cross the fine line between caution and expediency in advancing the freedoms of African Americans.

TRUMAN

Freedom for blacks seemed imperative to Harry Truman in the years following the end of World War II. For much more was at stake than the birthrights of American citizens:

> The support of desperate populations of battle ravaged countries must be won for the free way of life. We must have them as allies in our continuing struggle for the peaceful solution of the world's problems. They may surrender to the false security offered so temptingly by totalitarian regimes unless we can prove the superiority of democracy. Our case for democracy should be as strong as we can make it. It should rest on practical evidence that we have been able to put our own house in order.[30]

Truman did not choose these words to persuade a reluctant white audience to accept his concern for civil rights. He spoke these lines, rather, at a rally of the National Association for the Advancement of Colored People (NAACP) at the Lincoln Memorial in 1947. And Truman held to this view of civil rights throughout his presidency. "The peoples of the world are faced with the choice of freedom or enslavement," Truman repeated in the first presidential message on civil rights, delivered in February 1948. "If we wish to inspire the people of the world whose freedom is in jeopardy," Truman continued, "we must correct the remaining imperfections in our practice of democracy."[31]

Those remaining imperfections were, unfortunately for Truman, numerous and grievous when he came to office. From 1936 to 1946, at least forty-three African Americans had been lynched by white mobs nationwide, though principally in the Deep South, where in 1947 poll taxes were still in effect in seven states. During the Truman presidency, segregation–"Jim Crow"–on trains and buses and in theaters, hospitals, and elsewhere extended from the nation's capital to the Gulf of Mexico.[32] And in a number of widely publicized incidents, African American servicemen newly returned from war were set upon by white racists, including law-enforcement officials, in parts of the old Confederacy.[33] The plain necessity of civil rights protections, then, was not new when Harry Truman took office. But the Cold War was, and the pleas of the United States government to the nonwhite masses of the world to join the "free world" were met by the rejoinder of African Americans at home, who demanded *their* freedom now![34]

So Truman, the proud son of a Lincoln-hating admirer of the murderous Confederate hero William Quantrill, pursued civil rights–with caution.[35] Before the 1948 Democratic Convention, Truman limited his pursuit largely to oratory and the establishment of an advisory panel, the Committee on Civil Rights. The committee was established after the midterm congressional elections of 1946. Those elections were a debacle for the Democrats and suggested that "black voters, having switched to the Democratic party under the New Deal, were starting to drift back to their historic Republican moorings."[36]

Early in the next election season, Truman endorsed the committee's recommendations in a special message to Congress. Truman called on that occasion for numerous measures that the committee had recommended, including antilynching legislation, voting rights protections, the abolition of the poll tax, the desegregation of the military and the civil service, and a permanent Fair Employment Practices Commission (FEPC).[37] After this speech, and until the party's convention that summer, Truman temporized. He delayed issuing the promised desegregation orders–which he could have issued at any time, on his executive authority alone—and instead announced that he had instructed the secretary of defense to end discrimination (but not segregation) in the armed services. And when a controversy arose over discrimination in the National Guard, Truman "pushed for an agreement which would allow each state to decide its own racial policy." Against the request of the NAACP, furthermore, Truman spoke during this period at Girard College in Philadelphia, an institution then receiving national notoriety for its admissions ban against blacks. In seventy-three speeches on Truman's campaign tour of eighteen states in June, Truman mentioned civil rights only once.[38] "The strategy," according to a White House aide, "was to start with a bold measure and then temporize to pick up the right-wing forces. Simply stated, backtrack after the bang."[39]

What emboldened Truman to move beyond these cautious steps was the revolt of the northern liberals at the Democratic convention in July. The convention platform committee, with the support of the White House, at first endorsed a moderate civil rights plank echoing the 1944 document. When liberal delegates, headed by Minneapolis mayor Hubert Humphrey, threatened a roll-call vote, however, big-city politicians and union leaders broke from the White House. As a consequence, on the final vote for a more zealous civil rights measure, "the industrial states of the North and West defeated the South and the Truman loyalists" by a slim margin.[40]

The immediate consequence of the revolt of the "crackpots" was the rebellion of the Dixiecrats.[41] This rebellion has frequently been overrated. To begin with, only Mississippi and one-half of the Alabama delegation actually walked out of the convention.[42] And when the contest was over, the Dixiecrats, or States' Rights party, ran a poor third, with only 2 percent of the popular vote and thirty-nine electoral college votes to their credit. Few people in the nation were persuadable that, in the words of the States' Rights platform, federal enforcement of civil rights was "a totalitarian concept . . . unblushingly proposed."[43] As Robert Donovan, a leading historian of the Truman administration, writes, "[The] Dixiecrats turned out to be a ragtag band shunned by the South beyond Alabama, Mississippi, Louisiana, and South Carolina."[44]

After the convention, Truman and his aides had determined

readily that the Deep South reaction, though filled with vitriol, was unlikely to spread.[45] The convention debacle, Truman came to realize, had in fact presented his campaign with a fine opportunity to solidify its base in hotly contested and populous industrial states, without fear of a generalized white backlash, while also easing the embarrassment of America's racial antipathies. To most of the nation, after all, "America's racial problem was a Southern problem." Even in the South, the pragmatists typically had more clout than the States' Rights supporters.[46] Taking a more activist stance on this issue, therefore, seemed likely to win more votes than it would lose for the Democrats. Among those pressing this point of view on Truman were Clark Clifford, Truman's legal counsel and top political aide; James Rowe, a former New Deal lawyer and White House assistant; George Elsey, a Truman staffer; and Ed Flynn, the "boss of the Bronx."[47]

It would have taken "a considerable number of southern states to equal the importance of New York, Pennsylvania, and Delaware," Truman's advisers accurately reasoned.[48] Furthermore, A. Philip Randolph, the leader of the rail porters' union, was at the time threatening to lead African American males in an act of civil disobedience. Black men, Randolph asserted, would refuse to take up arms if called in the reinstated draft unless Truman issued his promised order desegregating the military. After the platform fight, and the reaction in the South, how could Truman remain passive, Randolph demanded to know. After all, even the Republican platform of that year proclaimed opposition "to the idea of racial segregation in the armed services."[49]

After the convention, and before the election, Truman issued his long-awaited executive orders banning discrimination in government employment and requiring equality of treatment in the armed services. Truman even became the first president to make a campaign appearance in Harlem, where he restated his Cold War theme.[50] "Democracy's answer to the challenge of totalitarianism," Truman said in Harlem, "is its promise of equal rights and equal opportunity for all mankind."[51]

Truman was lucky; his strategy worked. He won in one of the most stunning victories in American electoral history, and he won with more than two-thirds of the black vote, a higher percentage than Franklin Roosevelt ever attained. In crucial states such as Illinois and Ohio, it was the margin of victory.[52] But it is not so easy to say whether African Americans were therefore lucky too. Truman did not win a governing majority in the Congress, although the Democrats–unreconstructed and reconstructed alike–returned to majority party status in both houses. Little more was accomplished, furthermore, in the way of civil rights during Truman's one full term, and the party remained deeply divided. As a prime example of the futility of Truman's second-term civil rights measures, when the president created an FEPC-style organization during the Korean War, it was a pale shadow of the World War II agency, with but five professional staff members.[53]

Truman's goal was to free blacks from overt discrimination, at least in certain government-controlled settings. The president, we might say, was animated by a purely negative conception of freedom. Beyond being an expression of Truman's belief in simple decency and fairness, the higher purpose of securing freedom for African Americans was not to reconstitute the nation at home but to win respect for the United States abroad. Blacks and whites would presumably continue to go their separate ways but without the latter lynching the former. Lyndon Johnson, before he left office, spoke in a different way about civil rights. What he actually accomplished, however, was very much along the lines of what Harry Truman began: a cautious expansion of negative liberty.

JOHNSON

The civil rights law that President Lyndon Johnson took most pride in was the Voting Rights Act of 1965. Its origins, like the origins of Truman's agenda, were in part to be found in America's emergence as a world leader. Its roots were even more deeply sunk, though, in the personal aspirations of the president. To understand the meaning of the act requires an understanding, therefore, of President Johnson.

Publicly, Lyndon Johnson seldom missed an opportunity to praise Franklin D. Roosevelt. Privately, Johnson had another hero, a man he "especially admired . . . and defended," Huey P. Long. Long, the fabled "Kingfish" and near-dictator of Louisiana, had been preparing to run against Roosevelt for the presidency in 1936 when he was assassinated in Baton Rouge. Long, like Johnson, was spectacularly crude and extraordinarily driven. Both were also sincerely dedicated to using the powers of government to give things to people, especially to the poor.[54] But there were two chief stumbling blocks in the way of the Longs and Johnsons of the South. One was the "interests," the moneyed power of the Northeast, which, in league with the local aristocracy, exploited the workers of the South and stole the natural resources of what should have been prosperous states. The other was civil rights.

The South, Johnson believed (as had Truman), was living behind the times, distracting itself with the past while losing ground in the present.[55] In a campaign speech in New Orleans in 1964, Johnson explained the southern dilemma. A poor boy born in Mississippi, Johnson began, rose to become a United States senator from Texas. One night, late in his career, the senator sat up with Lyndon talking over the troubles of the South: the economic misery of the working folk, the arrogance of the high and mighty, and the exploitation of the land and its wealth by outsiders. The senator, Johnson said, wished he could go back to Mississippi and make "just one more Democratic speech." His home state, the senator lamented, had not heard a "real Democratic speech in thirty years." "All they ever hear at election time is nigra, nigra, nigra." So long as the South remained fixated on maintaining Jim Crow, the good life enjoyed more fully outside the region would remain forever out of the reach of the common southerner.[56] Huey Long, Johnson liked to remind his friends, "never niggered it."[57]

Lyndon Johnson could not say as much for himself when he became president. As a United States representative from the Texas hill country and an out-and-out New Dealer, Johnson had been able to steer clear of the race issue. The hill country is an area of German American immigrant communities and very few blacks. In the nineteenth century many German Americans had opposed slavery and the Confederacy, and in the twentieth century hill-country "Anglos," when bigoted, have tended to devote themselves to the "messkin," not the "nigra," problem.[58] But between the House of Representatives and Johnson's ultimate ambition lay the statewide office of senator. So in his first successful bid for the

Senate, in 1948, Johnson "niggered it," ranting against Truman's "so-called poll tax repeal bill" and his "so-called antilynching bill." Both, Johnson said, were really parts of "an effort to set up a police state in the guise of liberty."[59]

Johnson worked hard after that election to broaden his appeal as a potential presidential candidate. Thus, as Senate majority leader, he took the lead in passing the Civil Rights Act of 1957.[60] His role in that victory was sufficient to earn him the hatred of unreconstructed southerners (320). But it was not enough to win for Johnson what he longed for: the admiration of the "Kennedy liberals" and the "Harvards," who he thought would determine how history remembered him. And it was not enough to draw the Deep South into that confrontation with economic realities which Johnson also hoped to bring about.

To secure these twin aims, Johnson knew he would have to do more. When Kennedy was assassinated, Johnson got his chance. First came passage of a bill that President Kennedy had been lobbying for when he was killed. That bill became the Civil Rights Act of 1964, which banned discrimination in public transportation and accommodations. President Kennedy had been reluctant to recommend this bill to Congress but had finally done so in response to pressure from civil rights leaders.[61] Johnson's contribution was to seize the opportunity to turn the vote on this legislation into a test of Congress's devotion to a martyred head of state.[62] But the 1964 act was Kennedy's bill. It was also ineffective, as indeed all civil rights legislation had been, in addressing what Martin Luther King Jr. termed the "central front" of the civil rights struggle: voting rights.

The Voting Rights Act of 1965 was President Johnson's civil rights bill. Johnson laid the rhetorical groundwork for the act at the Democratic convention in August. In July 1964, Republican nominee Barry Goldwater had addressed the GOP convention in San Francisco. He had focused his remarks on freedom: the need for America to join with Europe in an "Atlantic civilization" that would "extend its hand" to all the nations of the world so that freedom might be "safeguard[ed] . . . from the force of tyranny abroad." In leading America along this path, the Republicans would be following, Goldwater had said, in the footsteps of

Abraham Lincoln.[63] Johnson, in his acceptance speech a month later, turned Goldwater's words back at him. The Democratic part in the contest of that year, Johnson announced, was to advance "the true cause of freedom." "For more than thirty years," Johnson said, the Democratic party had worked "to enlarge the freedom of man" by combating hunger, unemployment, and barriers to equal opportunity. Adapting the most famous slogan of Goldwater's campaign to his own purposes, the president next declared: "And every American knows in his heart that this is right!"[64]

Johnson's rhetorical parry of a Goldwater line was more than clever; it was sincere, and it goes a long way toward explaining the breakthrough success of the 1965 legislation. Voting is not a radical act in the United States. It is, indeed, often spoken of more as a civic responsibility than an individual liberty. As Johnson explained in his memoirs, "I feared that as long as these [black] citizens were alienated from the *rights* of the American system, they would continue to consider themselves outside the *obligations* of that system." Guaranteeing the right to vote, Johnson implied, is a socially responsible, conservative act.[65] Even in the South, this perspective was gaining strength by 1965. In 1963, while Alabama's governor, George Wallace, was promising "segregation forever," South Carolina's governor, Ernest (Fritz) Hollings, provided state police to oversee the integration of Clemson University. Georgia's governor, Carl Sanders, in the same year, barred George Wallace from addressing the Georgia legislature.[66] Things were, of course, very different in places like Selma, Alabama. But that is the point. The difference between Selma and the rest of the nation, even between the Deep South and the peripheral South, was great enough by the 1960s to make Selma's apartheid rules unconscionable throughout most of the nation.

Lyndon Johnson was fond of a Texas saying: "Don't try to kill the snake unless you've got the hoe in your hands."[67] The nationally televised events of "Bloody Sunday," March 7, 1965, put the hoe in the president's hands. When Selmans and civil rights leaders attempted a peaceful march, they were attacked by roughly one hundred state troopers, deputy sheriffs, and "volunteers." The public was outraged. After the attack, 52 percent of Americans said they believed "civil rights" to be the "most important problem facing the country." Sympathy demonstrations were staged from Bangor to Honolulu and even in New Orleans. On March 15, the president addressed the Congress and the nation on voting rights, and two days later he introduced the administration bill in the Congress.[68]

The Voting Rights Act of 1965, which targeted seven Deep South states and threatened to replace local with federal registrars, was effective. In Mississippi, the percentage of the black voting-age population which was registered rose to 59.8 percent by September 1967, up from 6.7 percent just a few years before.[69] By 1968 "massive black exclusion from electoral politics (0 to 24% registered) persisted in only fourteen counties," while blacks had become the majority of registered voters in three-fourths of Mississippi's counties, most of the Alabama "black belt," and southeastern and northeastern Georgia as well as parts of the South Carolina low country.[70]

AFTER THE VOTING RIGHTS ACT

The Voting Rights Act was, as Johnson said even before the law was passed, only the "end of the beginning" of modern controversy over the meaning of freedom in America.[71] The act had "opened the gates to opportunity," but more was to be demanded.[72] Johnson himself, we saw above, emphasized the positive obligation toward responsible civic behavior which he thought could be expected from blacks once they were guaranteed the liberty to vote. But what was the substance of this obligation? Johnson seemed to desire that blacks enter the fabled melting pot of a mostly white America. Many black civil rights leaders took a different view of the voting rights victory. They too saw negative and positive liberty as entwined, but they disagreed about the nature of the community that they had won the liberty to join.

The civil rights movement, according to Richard King, forged a consciousness and self-respect among blacks which was focused upon participation in black community life and black political struggle. Through participation, privation, and confrontation, blacks claimed negative freedoms that whites had long enjoyed.

But in the process, a transformation occurred. After that transformation, King suggests, assimilation in the melting pot did not look like a worthy use of freedom.[73]

To elaborate on this transformational perspective, we might say that although voting rights could not have been won if southern blacks had not had the courage to express the consciousness of their worth as individuals, individual empowerment and liberation paved the way for communal identity. Martin Luther King's understanding of this process was reminiscent of Lincoln's attempted teaching, only more bold. King, that is, believed that the ultimate goal of the movement he led was to achieve an inclusive, collective freedom of blacks *and* whites to do only that which is good. He expressed this conviction in his teasing promise to grant freedom to his oppressors. King preached that in confronting the American nation with its hypocrisy about being "the land of the free," the civil rights movement was winning freedom for the white majority as well as the black minority. "One day," King stated, "we shall win freedom, but not only for ourselves. We shall so appeal to your heart and conscience that we shall win *you* in the process, and our victory will be a double victory."[74]

There was, in addition, a third view of what sort of positive liberty negative liberty had made possible. This separatist vision was championed by a younger, more militant generation of activists, including Malcolm X, Huey Newton, and Stokely Carmichael. These men wished neither to join nor to transform white America. The programs of these leaders and their organizations, the Nation of Islam, the Black Panthers, and the Student Nonviolent Coordinating Committee, respectively, of course differed in their details. But they were in agreement on fundamentals. They aspired to black power, advanced through direct action against "white power" systems such as the police. Blacks in America, the militants asserted, could expect few benefits from peaceful coexistence with whites. They would be better off in voluntarily segregated communities and, even, in a new black nation.[75]

If politics were like a class in political science, the passage of the Voting Rights Act would have been followed by a discussion of the relative merits of each of these three perspectives. Does an assimilationist, transformational, or separatist vision best "complete" the negative liberty achieved by the 1965 legislation? That discussion never took place, or if it did, it never received a public hearing. One reason was Watts.

The riot in Watts began only six days after the Voting Rights Act was signed. By the time it was over, 34 persons had died, more than 1,000 had been injured, and over 1,000 buildings had been burned or vandalized. From that time to the end of Johnson's presidency, more than 250 cities were the sites of over 300 violent upheavals.[76] Many voters who had been appalled at the white violence in Selma were even more concerned by the black violence in the cities. The political consequences were made plain when, as Mark Stern notes, "*Newsweek* entitled a preelection article 'Politics: The White Backlash of 1966' and reported that for the first time since the early 1960s, whites now felt the administration was 'pushing civil rights too fast.'"[77]

The riots had many causes, but the federal guarantee of the voting rights of southern blacks was not among them. Nevertheless, they provided a disturbing backdrop to the further demands of the civil rights leaders. The separatist vision that came into its own at the same time as the riots was a nonstarter in American culture. The irony of voluntary separation as the cure for the ills of involuntary segregation was not popularly appreciated. The transformational vision of Martin Luther King has achieved some success, however, as opinion polls demonstrate an increased acceptance of racial integration.[78] But with regard to the meaning of freedom for African Americans in the 1990s, there appears to be no consensus over the positive implications of the negative freedom that blacks have achieved.

Some commentators and politicians stick with assimilationism. African Americans are now essentially freed from prejudice in the workplace, in the schools, and in politics. The pressing need now, they say, is for African Americans to demonstrate their commitment to the broader community into which they have at last been welcomed. That community is commonly defined as color-blind, in which equality of opportunity is formally guaranteed to all individuals. Others disagree, arguing for a modified transformational approach. Equality of results, from this perspective, is the only sure test of equality of opportunity. Freedom, these other voices say, obliges white Americans to demonstrate their commitment to persons of color by forsaking strict equality of opportunity to advance the equality of racial subcommunities. Clearly, while it is difficult to get people to agree on what freedom demands that they or others not do, it is much more so to bring people to agreement on what, if anything, freedom requires that they (or someone else) do.

CONCLUSION

Our ideas about freedom are indeterminate. Because freedom is a derivative idea, it can be no other way. The consequence in presidential politics is that, though demands for negative liberty are sometimes compelling, their achievement always represents a beginning, not an end, to controversy. Achieving freedom *from* constraints, though it can be tremendously costly in lives as well as risky to political careers, is easy compared with what always comes next: the necessity to determine through political conflict what the new freedoms are *for.* This paradox was apparent to President Lincoln.

Lincoln expressed two hopes about the legacy of freedom which his administration would leave behind. On the one hand, Lincoln expressed his conviction that justice required a renewed commitment to the laws, including the laws granting rights to freed blacks. Racial pride would prevent true assimilation, but mutual respect for the law might provide the foundation for the peaceful coexistence of blacks and whites. Each American owed to every other American a mature appreciation of the importance of the new laws and the ancient faith of equality upon which they were founded. Lincoln also expressed his hope, however, that northern free blacks might lead southern freed blacks in a mass exodus from the United States. Together, Lincoln's hopes did not add up to a coherent policy. They did, however, well express the president's pragmatic idealism. Though he accurately foresaw that his fame would rest on the people's memory of him as an emancipator, he pursued freedom with caution.

Harry Truman and Lyndon Johnson brought about more limited changes in policy. Still, those changes were bitterly contested, and the presidents had reason to be cautious. Like Lincoln, they were sincerely concerned for blacks in America. Also like Lincoln, however, they waited until it was expedient before they joined in the pursuit of new laws to guarantee the rights of blacks. At the moment that Lyndon Johnson pursued the Voting Rights Act, the public was highly favorable to such legislation, and Harry Truman might well have lost the election of 1948 had he not supported the demands that civil rights leaders were making. Unlike Lincoln, however, neither Truman nor Johnson seemed aware of the incompleteness of his achievement. Neither foresaw, that is, that once the demands of negative freedom had been met, the more controversial demands of positive liberty would come to the surface.

Today, there is probably less agreement on what our belief in freedom requires of us with regard to race than at any time since World War II. Will our presidents help resolve our differences? Perhaps, but if they are slow to act, we should not mistake a prudent caution and an unavoidable expediency for personal cowardice. Presidents cannot resolve for us the ambiguity inherent in our embrace of the ideal of freedom.

3

TO ESCAPE POWER, EMBRACE CHARISMA

I know America. I know the heart of America is good.
–President Richard M. Nixon
[speaking publicly]

You've got to be a little evil to understand those people out there.
–President Richard M. Nixon
[speaking privately]

PRESIDENT CLINTON'S CAT IS NAMED AFTER AN ARTICLE of clothing. His daughter attends an exclusive private school. He and his wife, Hillary, met as students at Yale Law School. The president, "Bill," is rumored to be a womanizer; he has a nagging weight problem, a fondness for junk food, and a half brother who fancies himself a singer. Chances are, if you were of voting age in 1993, you already knew all this. Why? Why is the relationship between the American people and their president so personal? Television and the decline of partisanship have been implicated as causes.[1] Another, overlooked factor in the development of an excessive familiarity in the president's relationship with the people is the famously American suspicion of power.

By investing the occupant of the Oval Office with the monarchical function of embodying the people, I mean to suggest, the public breaks down its resistance to power. Power is no longer to be feared because it is no longer emanating from an exterior source. When the monarchical president rules, he does not merely represent us or act as we might had we the chance to be in his position. He rather executes our desires and affirms our authorship of him. The president, the American common person's "strong arm against the world," thereby makes manifest our ruling passions, including the passion to rule.[2] Not the least of the difficulties arising from this ironic enlargement of presidential power is captured by what Harvey Mansfield terms "a comical maxim of human perception: 'Wounds and every other ill that man causes to himself spontaneously and through choice, hurt much less than those which are done to you by someone else.'"[3] As a consequence, once the people give themselves to a president, once they accept a particular man as their double, they are loath to let go. If nevertheless they do, the shock to the government can be immense. In this chapter, the Watergate and Iran-Contra affairs are examined in this context.

RICHARD NIXON AND WATERGATE

Richard Nixon understood the use of power. He may even have been, as he once said, one of only a handful of persons in America who did.[4] But he fell victim to it nonetheless. He did so, first of all, because—contrary to the contemporary image of the man—he established as president an intense and intimate symbolic association with millions of his compatriots.

Nixon called his supporters the "silent majority." They were, he said in Miami when accepting his party's nomination for the presidency in 1968, the "forgotten Americans, the non-shouters, the non-demonstrators . . . good people . . . decent people"; they worked and they saved; they paid their taxes and they cared.[5] Socially and culturally, Nixon's supporters were "middle American" traditionalists. Politically, they were the old Republican base plus the Solid South (which Truman and Johnson had unintentionally helped to drive out of the Democratic column by their support of civil rights), the farmers, and approximately half the Catholic, ethnic, and blue-collar voters of the cities.[6] For more than five years, Richard Nixon was not just their president; he was their champion in the cultural warfare of the late sixties and early seventies.

The sixties have a resonance in the American public memory unlike that of any other decade in this century. The delinquency of urban hooligans and the regional and ideological animosities that helped tear apart Lyndon Johnson's electoral coalition were not, of course, without parallel. So what was different about the sixties? Perhaps the most appropriate way to answer is with a verbal collage, adapting for the purpose of a historical sketch an art form that Robert Rauschenberg popularized in that decade.

–The Yippies were different. Their leader was Abbie Hoffman, a self-professed "action freak and anti-intellectual" who devoted himself to "monkey" warfare in the streets of New York.

–The National Mobilization Committee to End the War in Vietnam, or MOBE, was a force in the sixties. MOBE turned out hundreds of thousands to protest the war in April 1967 and to march on the Pentagon six months later.

–And there was a cop in Chicago who refused to permit Allard Lowenstein, a convention delegate from New York and a candidate for Congress, to enter the Democratic party's convention hall until he surrendered his copy of the *New York Times*.[7]

–There were also the race riots mentioned in the last chapter, many of them black pogroms against white merchants and their stores, white cops and their brutality, and, sometimes, white passersby. One hundred sixty-four riots took place in the first nine months of 1967 alone (362).

–The assassination of Martin Luther King Jr., John F. Kennedy, Robert Kennedy, Malcolm X.

–The race-baiting governor of Alabama, George C. Wallace, was something new (though certainly not without parallel). Wallace carried five southern states in the 1968 presidential election and polled 13.6 percent of the popular vote nationwide.

–There was also the women's movement and its internal struggles, including the putsch that sent Betty Friedan to *McCall's* and left Bella Abzug, Shirley Chisolm, and Gloria Steinem in control of the National Women's Political Caucus.[8]

–There were, most generally, "apocalyptic events" and the "collective willingness to suspend one's better judgment," resulting in a "revolutionary [and counterrevolutionary] mood."[9]

Richard Nixon understood: "We are caught in war, wanting peace," he said, speaking of both domestic and foreign events. Nixon's greatest ambition, he said time and again, was to be the "peace maker."[10]

When he first took office, Nixon hoped that the sixties, the "long night of the American spirit," were ending (228). Eight months into his presidency, the liberal establishment proved him wrong. That was when, as Nixon saw it, *it* declared war on *him.* In October and November of his first year in office, massive antiwar demonstrations took place just beyond the White House gates. Referring to the demonstrations and, most pointedly, the media coverage of them, the respected reporter David Broder wrote in the *Washington Post* that it was "becoming more obvious with every passing day that the men and the movement that broke Lyndon Johnson's authority in 1968 [were] out to break Richard M. Nixon in 1969." The protests and their coverage were, Broder concluded, "an effort of the intellectual elite to obliterate the 1968 election."[11] The president subsequently decided to go on the offensive, declaring himself on the side of the Center-Right in the ongoing culture war.

Nixon made his declaration in a nationally televised speech delivered on November 3, 1969. In the speech, the president explained his policy of Vietnamization–cautiously to withdraw American troops from the war, to be replaced by South Vietnamese forces–and provided details of his ongoing negotiations with the North Vietnamese. If his policy was not supported, Nixon asserted, it would be proof of the nation's destruction at the hands of the liberal establishment, the hippies, and the freaks. "If a vocal minority, however fervent its cause," was to prevail over "reason and the will of the majority," Nixon warned, the nation had "no future as a free society." Consequently, Nixon implored "the great silent majority of [his] fellow Americans" to support him. That majority had a vital task, Nixon went on to suggest. If the silent majority was solid in its support of Nixon, the shouters and demonstrators and liberals could be defeated. Their defeat was imperative. "Let us understand," the president remarked, "North Vietnam cannot defeat or humiliate the United States. Only Americans can do that."[12]

The response was swift and positive. In every single category of respondent, from the "over fifty" and "under thirty" age groups to the union and nonunion workers, white and nonwhite, Protestant and Catholic, approval of the president increased after this speech. From a 56 percent approval rating at the end of October, Nixon's average approval rating went up to 67 percent in mid-November and was above 70 percent among men, midwesterners, southerners, Republicans, Protestants, and the college-educated.[13] It was the second-biggest jump (in either direction) in Nixon's approval rating during his presidency; the people were taking sides.[14]

Fully three-quarters of the voting-age public told pollsters that they thought they belonged to Nixon's silent majority. "A Political Masterpiece," declared the *New Republic.* And it was not a fluke. Nixon's rapport with the people was strong for most of his time in office. George C. Edwards concludes a study of Nixon's popular support with the observation that "until the Watergate scandal broke, [Richard Nixon] experienced a significant degree of support from the public" (170). As the campaign slogan had it, Nixon was "the one": the one who stood up against the "bums blowing up the campuses," the dissenters, intellectuals, and news commentators. When a group of construction workers in New York City witnessed an antiwar demonstrator urinate on a statue of George Washington, they came down from their scaffolding and (why be coy?) beat the crap out of the protestors. The president invited the hard hats to the White House.[15]

Nixon's "oneness" with the silent majority was both his strength and his weakness. In celebrating the tactics of the hard hats, as in his and his vice president's attacks on the media, Nixon deepened his significance as a symbol of certainty for millions of Americans. He was, Howard Stein has written, like that other flawed antihero (or hero) of the time, Archie Bunker:

> Those who secretly or openly cheer Archie on know of his impotence, his desperation for control, and they hold on the same way he does, holding on defiantly . . . desperately. . . . [W]ith the world (inner and outer) slipping more and more out of their grasp and control, they take increasingly desperate steps to wrest back the control that has been taken away, or to protect that which they fear will be alienated.

The result, for Archie and the rest of us, is the resort "to virtually any tactics to assure safety, security and quiet." "By knowing Archie Bunker," Stein believes, "one can understand why Watergate was not only possible, but tacitly condoned and endorsed."[16]

Stein, I think, is on to something, though he perhaps understates his case. Nixon was an even more attractive figure for traditionalist Americans than was Archie Bunker. For unlike Bunker, who had no true recourse against his "meatheaded" antagonists, Nixon had the power of the presidency at his disposal. When he used it to praise the men who beat up the "bums," the silent majority could take vicarious pleasure in the skull-cracking antics of the patriots in the hard hats. Unlike Archie, the construction workers actually did something about (or at least to) their enemies.

In the summer of 1971, after the White House's attention had already turned to the reelection of the president, Nixon escalated his use of power. He did so in response to a number of events that he later insisted were threats to national security. The most prominent such event was Daniel Ellsberg's leak to the *New York Times* of a classified history of United States involvement in Vietnam. In the judgment of Charles Colson, at the time a White House strategist and self-described "flag-waving, kick-em-in-the-nuts, anti-press, anti-liberal Nixon fanatic," the White House "passed a crossroads" in its reaction to the release of the Pentagon Papers.[17] And indeed, after Ellsberg's revelations, Nixon approved the creation of the infamous unit to plug leaks (the "plumbers") which a year later was caught burglarizing the offices of Democratic national chairman Larry O'Brien.

The reaction to the Watergate break-in did not at first harm Nixon. This was so even though one of the five burglars was James McCord, a security consultant to Nixon's campaign organization, the unfortunately named Committee to Re-Elect the President

White House instructed the FBI to "take" the headquarters of the former special prosecutor. Television cameras relayed to the nation dramatic footage of plain-clothed and uniformed officers evicting the public's sleuths from their offices and sealing off their building. The response included a half-million telegrammed expressions of outrage. The people were now at the *receiving* end of presidential power, and they lashed back as the protestors had.

Nixon himself knew it was all over on July 23, 1974, just two weeks before resigning office. On that day, the president talked to George Wallace, the man whose admirers Nixon had rallied to the ranks of the silent majority. He had telephoned Wallace to ask his help in dissuading Alabama representative Walter Flowers from voting for impeachment. When Wallace replied that it would be inappropriate for him to attempt any such dissuasion, the president reportedly turned to Al Haig (who had replaced Haldeman as chief of staff) and said: "Well, Al, there goes the presidency" (505).

"My president is a liar." With this revelation, this hurt, the spell was broken. To resist the authority of a king, John Locke explained in *The Second Treatise of Government*, was unlawful treason. But: "When a King has dethroned himself, and put himself in a state of war with his people, what shall hinder them from prosecuting him who is no King?"[25] By lying to the people about his role in the coverup, and by turning his power against the people themselves, Nixon dethroned himself and suffered the consequences.

RONALD REAGAN AND IRAN-CONTRA

"My president is a liar." Could this not also be said of Ronald Reagan? On July 8, 1985, President Reagan, in a speech before the American Bar Association, called Iran part of a confederation of "outlaw states run by the strangest collection of misfits, Looney Tunes and squalid criminals since the advent of the Third Reich." One month later, the president met with his National Security Council (NSC) to discuss an indirect arms-for-hostages swap with Iranian "moderates." On September 15, hostage Benjamin Wier was released in exchange for more than five hundred American

(CREEP). The major networks and the papers, especially the *Washington Post*, gave the story prominent coverage, and Senator George McGovern, the Democrat's hapless presidential candidate in 1972, even featured the break-in in one of his TV spots late in the campaign.[18] Still, Nixon won handily, rolling up a huge victory. Nixon's reelection was, moreover, a demonstration of personal, not partisan, support. In 1968, Nixon had earned the dubious distinction of being the first elected president since Zachary Taylor whose party had not also carried at least one branch of Congress in the same year as the president's first election. In his reelection, Republican candidates for Congress found that Nixon's coattails had grown no longer in four years. The net effect of four years of Republican control of the presidency, from 1969 to 1973, was a gain of zero seats in the House and the loss of one in the Senate.

Looking ahead to his second term, the president entertained some grandiose ambitions: to "reform, replace, or circumvent" institutions in American life which were not allied with the silent majority; to combat what he characterized as "fashionable negativism" and an "underlying loss of will" among American elites. Nixon decided that in his second term he would reach further and grasp harder than he had yet dared for control of the executive bureaucracy and even contest the congressional prerogative of appropriations. He would, furthermore, deinstitutionalize these conflicts, so that "the people" would see not merely the president battling the Congress or the cabinet or the press but their champion overwhelming the forces of the "New Minority."[19]

Conventional wisdom holds that Nixon was done in by hubris. In grasping for power, Nixon made too many enemies. They therefore took the opportunity that Watergate offered them to attack the president. But this explanation only begs the question: Why did Nixon not prevail against his opponents? Two reasons stand out. First, there is the Fiesco Factor. "The Moor has done his work, the Moor may go." So says a character in Friedrich Schiller's play *Fiesco*.[20] "The labor was worth its hire" expresses the same attitude in more familiar language. In the first month of his second term, Nixon signed the accords that would end American involvement in the war in Vietnam and that would bring home all

American prisoners of war. The immediate reaction was relief and gratitude. The president's approval ratings went to their highest level, 67 percent nationwide. The next month, Nixon's ratings began a precipitate decline, reaching below the 50 percent mark by April, below 40 percent by July, and below 30 percent by the end of the year.[21] Once the war accords had been signed, Nixon was a discomforting reminder of the war and its divisiveness; the peacemaker was an embarrassing reminder of war.

Second, and this is perhaps related to the first factor in his demise, Nixon was caught in a lie that he told not to himself (as did Reagan, as we shall see) but to that same silent majority whose trust he had earlier earned. Watergate was, initially, a sort of black comedy: a "third-rate burglary" was how Nixon put it. The press obligingly picked up on Nixon's lead, asking: Who were these clowns? What were they looking for?[22]

On March 23, 1973, the questions asked in the press began to change to the detriment of Nixon's bond with the people. On that day, twenty-four hours before Judge John J. Sirica was to hand down sentences on the Watergate burglars, McCord broke his silence. In a letter that the judge read in open court, McCord asserted that political pressure was being exerted upon him and the other defendants and that "others" had been responsible for the crime. This revelation changed the story line from one of a "bungled burglary" to a "coverup," from a comedy to a mystery. The press, as it gained access to high-ranking officials around the president, began its remorseless quest for the answer to the famous question: What did the president know, and when did he know it?[23] This question was posed first in public by Senator Howard Baker, the ranking Republican on one of the committees investigating the break-in. As media analysts Gladys and Kurt Lang comment:

> To have asked in more straightforward fashion whether the President, and not Dean [John Dean, Nixon's counsel, who gave damning testimony against the president] might have been lying was unthinkable. Senators no less than most Americans regard the office with almost sacred awe. Yet from here on, the veracity of the President . . . was ever more deeply an issue. (78)

Among those most engrossed with the unfolding st
sons who had voted for Nixon in 1972. Such peopl
Langs, were among those "least inhibited in their e
shock and outrage" (87–88).

In the White House, Nixon knew that his standi
people was at risk. Shortly after McCord's letter was r
Sirica, but before Baker asked his famous question,
on the telephone with his chief of staff. In that convers
told Haldeman, "Despite all the polls . . . I think there
of a lot of people out there, and from what I've seen . .
to believe. That's the point, isn't it?" (46). Nixon was
time. But with the revelation in the summer of 1973 c
House's taping apparatus, the pressure from the pub
media to hear those tapes and settle the mystery was
ing. And the tapes, of course, would prove fatal to Nix
The tapes had recorded Nixon as he discussed with De
ment of hush money to the burglars and as he sought
for the CIA to halt the FBI investigation into the brea
thing Nixon had straightforwardly insisted in a natio
vised appearance that he had never done. "I am clos
wrote conservative columnist James Kilpatrick when
were finally released. "My president is a liar. I wish
crook instead."[24]

Nixon was in a no-win situation. If he released the
would expose his lies. But in trying to prevent their relea
risked alienating his supporters. The low point for the
as he struggled with this dilemma, came in the "Satur
Massacre" of October 20, 1973. On that date, Nixon, in a
quash the special prosecutor's efforts to make him revea
tents of his tapes, ordered his attorney general, Elliot Ri
to fire the special prosecutor, Archibald Cox. Richardson
because he could not comply with the president's orde
violating a pledge he had made in his Senate confirmati
ings. Minutes later, Richardson's deputy, William Ruck
also quit rather than carry out the president's command.
the number-three person in the department, Solicitor
Robert Bork, fired Cox. Immediately upon Cox's remo

missiles, delivered to Iran through Israel. Still, White House spokesman Larry Speakes insisted that the United States was firmly opposed "to negotiations with terrorists or concessions to them." On November 15, Reagan's national security adviser, Robert McFarlane, conveyed to the Israeli go-between the president's authorization for further arms sales to Iran. And on December 5, 1985, January 6, 1986, and January 17, 1986, the president signed "findings" required by law to initiate covert operations. These findings made clear the arms-for-hostages nature of the Iranian operation.[26]

The duplicity continued once a Lebanese newspaper exposed the operation in November 1986. In his first public statement on the subject, Reagan denied news reports that the United States had sold arms to Iran. In a presidential address to the nation, Reagan insisted that the United States had not swapped arms "or anything else" for the release of hostages. After further public revelations, the appointment of an independent counsel, and the empanelment of a Senate select committee, a House select committee, and a special presidential commission, Reagan continued to resist pressure (and the advice of former president Nixon) to "come clean" and beg the forgiveness of the nation.[27] In his most forthright statement on the event, the president explained that he had intended to open a dialogue with moderates in Iran, looking ahead, as presidents are supposed to do, to the future of the region. He had therefore authorized shipments of arms to persons within the Iranian government who claimed to have influence over the terrorists holding Americans hostage in Lebanon. "A few months ago, I told the American people I did not trade arms for hostages. My heart and my best intentions still tell me that is true, but the facts and the evidence tell me it is not."[28]

If this was a confession, it was of a peculiar kind. Reagan acknowledged not a fault, ignorance, but a virtue, compassion. As Reagan revealed later in this address, he let his "preoccupation with the hostages intrude into areas where it didn't belong. The image–the reality–of Americans in chains burdened [his] thoughts."[29] As Roger Rosenblatt wrote in *Time* magazine, "In the Iran transaction he [Reagan] apparently felt the plight of the hostages as one would feel the plight of one's family in danger."[30]

Compassion, of course, is a quality Americans admire in themselves. Because they so thoroughly identified with Ronald Reagan the person, it was easy for them to extend to him their sympathy, rather than express to him their outrage, once the facts of the Iran half of the affair became evident.

As for the Contra half of the story, we know that some of the profits from the sale of arms were sent to the Contras in Nicaragua, in violation of the Boland amendment prohibiting U.S. government support of the anti-Sandinista forces. What we do not know is whether the president lied about his lack of knowledge of the diversion. President Reagan never acknowledged knowing about this operation, and no evidence has been uncovered to the contrary. There was no "smoking gun." This was an important difference between Watergate and Iran-Contra, though I do not think it explains their dissimilar outcomes. But before delving further into this story, it is necessary to examine the relationship that existed between the American people and Ronald Reagan at the time the scandal broke.

The defining moment in the public's relationship to President Nixon was his speech invoking the support of the "silent majority." The pivotal event in President Reagan's assumption of office was different; he was shot. The public's affinity for Ronald Reagan assumed mythic proportions when he survived an assassination attempt just months into his administration. This event, according to Haynes Johnson, elevated Reagan "into a place in the affections of his fellow citizens that he never lost during his years as president." "It signaled," Johnson continues, "the breaking of the skein of bad luck that had plagued the nation and its leaders for nearly twenty years."[31] Not only did he survive, of course, but he cracked jokes with his wife and the doctors on the way into surgery. ("Honey, I forgot to duck." "I hope you guys are Republicans.") The Great Communicator thereby communicated not only good fortune but a much-admired optimism and courage as well. Ronald Reagan was the nation's good luck charm.

Survey researchers concur, in part, with these impressions. President Reagan's personal likability–the proportion of respondents in national surveys who reported a "favorable" opinion of the president "as a person"–was very high and highly stable over his two terms. The high point (81%) on this scale for Reagan came just after his reelection; the low point (72%) was registered in the summer of 1987, in the midst of the Iran-Contra congressional hearings. When Reagan left office, his personal approval stood at 79 percent, one point higher than the first rating reported for his eight years in office.[32]

The proportion of respondents who approved of Reagan's *performance* as president was less stable. Reagan, in fact, took office with the lowest approval rating of any prior president for whom such data are available, and his average approval of 54 percent over two terms puts him in the middle of the seven presidents from Eisenhower through Reagan.[33] Reagan's public, furthermore, was the most polarized of any president since national survey research began. In support of Ronald Reagan, nonunion workers lined up against their union peers, men against women, and whites against blacks. Support for Reagan was significantly higher among the former group in each of these pairings.[34] On the basis of such evidence, Martin Wattenberg concluded that since the 1950s, "no victorious presidential candidate has been more intensely disliked among his opponents, greeted with more doubts among his supporters, and hence more unpopular overall with the voters than Ronald Reagan."[35] Barry Sussman similarly found in his study of opinion polls that even at its height, Reagan's public approval was "fragile" and based on "superficial feelings."[36]

What is to be made of this confusion of data? To make sense of the numbers, as an initial observation, we are going to have to go beyond them. The relationship between a president and the public is, after all, just that, a relationship. It would make no more sense to reduce the president-public relationship to a percentage point than to do the same thing to the relationship between a father and his children. What if, for instance, 64 percent of American children approved of the job their fathers were doing in 1955, whereas in 1993 only 51 percent of children reported their approval? Such findings are indicators, hints really, that something worth reflecting upon is going on. But what might that something be? With respect to Ronald Reagan, what did his comparatively low performance ratings mean? What was his symbolic value to those Americans who approved of him as president and, especially, to those who disapproved of the "job he was doing" but liked him nonetheless?

"I always had the feeling," writes Reagan speechwriter Peggy Noonan in her White House memoirs, "[that] he came from a sad house and he thought it was his job to cheer everyone up."[37] At this task, he was truly the master. Once, Noonan relates, Mike Deaver, Reagan's image manager in the first term, took aside White House aide Richard Darman and said: "Listen, Darman, I don't care what else you do but make sure you do this: Get that face on television. This is a face that when a baby sees it, the baby smiles" (149–50). And the baby's parents must often have smiled too. As president, Reagan at one point received eight million letters a year, twice the presidential average. Each year Reagan answered thousands of these letters personally, "with the same kind of care and respect that he gave to a letter from Thatcher or Kohl." Noonan continues:

> People thought he was their friend. They'd send him pictures of themselves and their families. The original letters would come back to Ann [Higgins, who ran the president's mail operation], but she noticed he always removed the pictures. They started showing up in the pockets of his jackets and coats and in the drawers of the lamp tables in the residence. (171)

"People thought he was their friend." And he, apparently, thought of them as family. As a consequence, both within the White House and in the public spaces beyond, "the idea of Reagan ruled" (166). The idea of Reagan was the idea of a truly likable national patriarch, who loved America and comforted its worried inhabitants, helping them not to think unpleasant thoughts about unsettling realities. It was "morning again in America."[38]

The duplicity of Reagan's strategic opening to Iran hurt the people who felt a sense of kinship with him. The 21-point plummet in the president's approval rating in the month after the revelations of November 1986 was the largest such drop ever recorded for a president.[39] It was a difficult moment. "For the first time in my life," Reagan recalls in his memoirs, "people didn't believe me."[40] (A whopping 90% of them did not, according to a *Newsweek* poll taken at the time.)[41] But, unlike Watergate, it was only a momentary panic, which subsided before approval ratings reached

(CREEP). The major networks and the papers, especially the *Washington Post*, gave the story prominent coverage, and Senator George McGovern, the Democrat's hapless presidential candidate in 1972, even featured the break-in in one of his TV spots late in the campaign.[18] Still, Nixon won handily, rolling up a huge victory. Nixon's reelection was, moreover, a demonstration of personal, not partisan, support. In 1968, Nixon had earned the dubious distinction of being the first elected president since Zachary Taylor whose party had not also carried at least one branch of Congress in the same year as the president's first election. In his reelection, Republican candidates for Congress found that Nixon's coattails had grown no longer in four years. The net effect of four years of Republican control of the presidency, from 1969 to 1973, was a gain of zero seats in the House and the loss of one in the Senate.

Looking ahead to his second term, the president entertained some grandiose ambitions: to "reform, replace, or circumvent" institutions in American life which were not allied with the silent majority; to combat what he characterized as "fashionable negativism" and an "underlying loss of will" among American elites. Nixon decided that in his second term he would reach further and grasp harder than he had yet dared for control of the executive bureaucracy and even contest the congressional prerogative of appropriations. He would, furthermore, deinstitutionalize these conflicts, so that "the people" would see not merely the president battling the Congress or the cabinet or the press but their champion overwhelming the forces of the "New Minority."[19]

Conventional wisdom holds that Nixon was done in by hubris. In grasping for power, Nixon made too many enemies. They therefore took the opportunity that Watergate offered them to attack the president. But this explanation only begs the question: Why did Nixon not prevail against his opponents? Two reasons stand out. First, there is the Fiesco Factor. "The Moor has done his work, the Moor may go." So says a character in Friedrich Schiller's play *Fiesco*.[20] "The labor was worth its hire" expresses the same attitude in more familiar language. In the first month of his second term, Nixon signed the accords that would end American involvement in the war in Vietnam and that would bring home all

American prisoners of war. The immediate reaction was relief and gratitude. The president's approval ratings went to their highest level, 67 percent nationwide. The next month, Nixon's ratings began a precipitate decline, reaching below the 50 percent mark by April, below 40 percent by July, and below 30 percent by the end of the year.[21] Once the war accords had been signed, Nixon was a discomforting reminder of the war and its divisiveness; the peacemaker was an embarrassing reminder of war.

Second, and this is perhaps related to the first factor in his demise, Nixon was caught in a lie that he told not to himself (as did Reagan, as we shall see) but to that same silent majority whose trust he had earlier earned. Watergate was, initially, a sort of black comedy: a "third-rate burglary" was how Nixon put it. The press obligingly picked up on Nixon's lead, asking: Who were these clowns? What were they looking for?[22]

On March 23, 1973, the questions asked in the press began to change to the detriment of Nixon's bond with the people. On that day, twenty-four hours before Judge John J. Sirica was to hand down sentences on the Watergate burglars, McCord broke his silence. In a letter that the judge read in open court, McCord asserted that political pressure was being exerted upon him and the other defendants and that "others" had been responsible for the crime. This revelation changed the story line from one of a "bungled burglary" to a "coverup," from a comedy to a mystery. The press, as it gained access to high-ranking officials around the president, began its remorseless quest for the answer to the famous question: What did the president know, and when did he know it?[23] This question was posed first in public by Senator Howard Baker, the ranking Republican on one of the committees investigating the break-in. As media analysts Gladys and Kurt Lang comment:

> To have asked in more straightforward fashion whether the President, and not Dean [John Dean, Nixon's counsel, who gave damning testimony against the president] might have been lying was unthinkable. Senators no less than most Americans regard the office with almost sacred awe. Yet from here on, the veracity of the President . . . was ever more deeply an issue. (78)

Among those most engrossed with the unfolding story were persons who had voted for Nixon in 1972. Such people, report the Langs, were among those "least inhibited in their expressions of shock and outrage" (87–88).

In the White House, Nixon knew that his standing with the people was at risk. Shortly after McCord's letter was read by Judge Sirica, but before Baker asked his famous question, Nixon spoke on the telephone with his chief of staff. In that conversation, Nixon told Haldeman, "Despite all the polls . . . I think there's still a hell of a lot of people out there, and from what I've seen . . . they want to believe. That's the point, isn't it?" (46). Nixon was right, for a time. But with the revelation in the summer of 1973 of the White House's taping apparatus, the pressure from the public and the media to hear those tapes and settle the mystery was overwhelming. And the tapes, of course, would prove fatal to Nixon's career. The tapes had recorded Nixon as he discussed with Dean the payment of hush money to the burglars and as he sought to arrange for the CIA to halt the FBI investigation into the break-in, something Nixon had straightforwardly insisted in a nationally televised appearance that he had never done. "I am close to tears," wrote conservative columnist James Kilpatrick when the tapes were finally released. "My president is a liar. I wish he were a crook instead."[24]

Nixon was in a no-win situation. If he released the tapes, he would expose his lies. But in trying to prevent their release, he also risked alienating his supporters. The low point for the president, as he struggled with this dilemma, came in the "Saturday Night Massacre" of October 20, 1973. On that date, Nixon, in an effort to quash the special prosecutor's efforts to make him reveal the contents of his tapes, ordered his attorney general, Elliot Richardson, to fire the special prosecutor, Archibald Cox. Richardson resigned because he could not comply with the president's order without violating a pledge he had made in his Senate confirmation hearings. Minutes later, Richardson's deputy, William Ruckelshaus, also quit rather than carry out the president's command. Finally, the number-three person in the department, Solicitor General Robert Bork, fired Cox. Immediately upon Cox's removal, the

White House instructed the FBI to "take" the headquarters of the former special prosecutor. Television cameras relayed to the nation dramatic footage of plain-clothed and uniformed officers evicting the public's sleuths from their offices and sealing off their building. The response included a half-million telegrammed expressions of outrage. The people were now at the *receiving* end of presidential power, and they lashed back as the protestors had.

Nixon himself knew it was all over on July 23, 1974, just two weeks before resigning office. On that day, the president talked to George Wallace, the man whose admirers Nixon had rallied to the ranks of the silent majority. He had telephoned Wallace to ask his help in dissuading Alabama representative Walter Flowers from voting for impeachment. When Wallace replied that it would be inappropriate for him to attempt any such dissuasion, the president reportedly turned to Al Haig (who had replaced Haldeman as chief of staff) and said: "Well, Al, there goes the presidency" (505).

"My president is a liar." With this revelation, this hurt, the spell was broken. To resist the authority of a king, John Locke explained in *The Second Treatise of Government*, was unlawful treason. But: "When a King has dethroned himself, and put himself in a state of war with his people, what shall hinder them from prosecuting him who is no King?"[25] By lying to the people about his role in the coverup, and by turning his power against the people themselves, Nixon dethroned himself and suffered the consequences.

RONALD REAGAN AND IRAN-CONTRA

"My president is a liar." Could this not also be said of Ronald Reagan? On July 8, 1985, President Reagan, in a speech before the American Bar Association, called Iran part of a confederation of "outlaw states run by the strangest collection of misfits, Looney Tunes and squalid criminals since the advent of the Third Reich." One month later, the president met with his National Security Council (NSC) to discuss an indirect arms-for-hostages swap with Iranian "moderates." On September 15, hostage Benjamin Wier was released in exchange for more than five hundred American the dangerously low levels that Nixon faced, or even the levels of Reagan's first-term recession. What saved Reagan, I think, and the crucial difference between Watergate and Iran-Contra, was that Reagan never seemed to have turned his grant of power from the people back at the people. For this reason, the bond forged between Reagan and his admirers remained firm, and was perhaps even strengthened, once the public learned the details of the affair.

Fittingly, the man who divulged the facts of Iran-Contra was not a stolid young attorney, like John Dean, but a mawkish marine officer. Lieutenant Colonel Oliver (Ollie) North was Ronald Reagan's kind of guy. Reagan even called him a "national hero." North, too, acted for us, not to us or against us. He, and his superior, national security adviser John Poindexter, did not need to ask our permission, any more than they needed to ask Reagan's, for the crucial diversion operation. In the decade when "the idea of Reagan ruled," they simply knew that by supporting "freedom fighters" against "communists," they were doing right by America. And, indeed, public support for the president's stand in Nicaragua increased dramatically in response to North's teary-eyed explanations of his mission, televised (in Watergate style) live on all the major networks.

North, an aide to the National Security Council who had operational control over both halves of the Iran-Contra affair, testified before Congress wearing his marine uniform. He was, according to those present, a consummate actor. His part was that of the unappreciated but stoic warrior for a just cause, doing his work, which was also the work of the president, the nation, and God. He had done all he could to help the brave and good men of the Contra army and to win the release of Americans held hostage abroad. Yes, he admitted, he had used funds from the "Enterprise" to erect a simple fence around his modest suburban home. But that was to protect his wife and children from the clutches of a diabolical terrorist who had threatened their lives. Were such acts, big and small, illegal? North was asked. Had he lied about his activities up to this point? "You have to weigh lies against lives," North replied.

Haynes Johnson captured well the impact of North's performance. "The country was enthralled by North. Here, at last, was a genuine hero. Even the childishness and bungling that typified much of his and the Enterprise's dealings were cloaked with a kind of exuberant innocence. . . . It was a remarkable show."[42] Indeed it was; the July 9, 1986, edition of the *Washington Post*, according to the count of two senators involved in the hearings, contained twenty-three pictures of North.[43] And on the last day of his testimony, when committee counsel Arthur Liman returned after a midday recess, he went to the hearing room to find "what appeared to be the entire Senate police force lined up before the committee platforms. Along with them were other committee functionaries. In front of them was a Senate photographer. And there, standing in the center, posing like a president, was Oliver North."[44]

Like a president, or at least like one particular president, a man whose defining stance was the photographic pose, Oliver North acted for us on a global stage. His actions, and by extension those of his president, were "innocent" as a consequence. It did not matter that some of his and the president's actions were perhaps stupid (selling arms to alleged moderates in a fanatical state) or that others were illegal (the diversion of funds from those same sales).[45] It was all, arguably, for a good cause; it was all good, clean fun. Gary Larson, author of the comic strip "The Far Side," lampooned the whole affair in a panel depicting two teenaged boys in jeans and T-shirts sitting before the raised dais of a congressional hearing room. "Well, sir, at the time, me and my brother were trying to solve the secret of Pirate's Cove. We had no idea where the whole thing would lead," says one of the youths. The caption reads: "Testifying before a Senate subcommittee, the Hardy Boys crack the Iran-Contra scandal." It is difficult to imagine such a lighthearted riposte to the Watergate affair.

CONCLUSION

Perhaps Nixon was right in both the quotations with which this chapter began. The American people are both good and "a little evil." They enjoy a righteous crusade and a good fight. But one thing "those people out there" do not enjoy is being forced to confront unpleasant truths. The necessity of government is one of the truths which has most consistently troubled Americans. In their quest for relief from the imperative of locating and building up power within the state, the people have responded by anointing their presidents with the monarchical license to act in their stead. So long as the public perceives no serious train of abuses of this privilege, the "king" remains a king and is granted wide latitude. But if the king breaks his bond with the people, they may withdraw their gift. The king will then find little protection in his office.

Richard Nixon was thus built up and cut down by people who thought of him in the intimate terms of kin(g)ship. Nixon acted out for the silent majority its impulses and angers. When the overarching purpose toward which these tasks had been directed was achieved–when the peace treaty with Vietnam was signed–it was as if the people awoke, ashamed, from an evil dream. To erase the memories of fratricide, they committed parricide.

Ronald Reagan also experienced the classic tragic sequence of elevation and fall. But in Reagan's case, the final act was different. Nixon, at the end of his administration, was excluded from the community that had at first embraced him. Reagan was sent into only a temporary exile; before he left office, the people accepted him back into their hearts. Reagan's presidency thus followed the pattern not of Shakespearean tragedy but comedy. He ended his administration as he had begun it, with evocations of the unity of the people. He was once again their head of state, their embodiment, their king.

Reagan, we might say, understood the source of his power better than did Nixon. He acted always as if he knew that the people may thrill to the vicarious exercise of power, but only so long as it is directed at the enemies of the community. Nixon, in turning power back on the people themselves, exposed himself as only a politician after all.

It would be better, I think, if Americans were to keep in mind that all their presidents are politicians after all. The difficulty is that because he is head of state, the president's significance as an icon can overwhelm us, and him. The symbolic weight of the office is too much for some presidents. Insofar as it invites the public to indulge in fantasies, it is also too much for us to bear without more conscious and critical consideration.

4

THE PRESIDENT IS OUR PROPERTY

THE FRAMERS OF THE CONSTITUTION DID NOT INTEND for the presidency to be the property of the people. Indeed, the people, as a group, were not intended to lay claim to any part of the government. Only in ratifying and subsequently amending the Constitution itself were "we the people" to speak with a single voice in government. In *Federalist* paper 63, James Madison boasted, in fact, that the "true distinction" between ancient republics of antiquity and the American system of governance would lie "in the total exclusion of the people in their collective capacity, from any share in the latter."[1] One political theorist goes so far as to suggest that in circumscribing the popular capacity to take collective action, the framers meant to hoodwink the people. The framers "rendered the democratic vocabulary of popular sovereignty harmless," Joshua Miller complains, "by invoking a fictitious people who could not possibly act together." They "ascribed all power to a mythical entity that could never meet, never deliberate, never take action."[2]

If Miller is correct about the framers' intent, however, the joke turned out to be on them. For the people adopted a possessive attitude toward its political apparatus, laying claim especially to the presidency. In the passing of a single generation, the presidency became like those institutions of antiquity which Madison proclaimed had no counterpart in the United States, the ephori and tribunes of Sparta and Rome, "elected by the whole body of the people, and considered as the representatives of the people, almost in their plenipotentiary capacity."[3] To see what happened, and to what effect, we will return to the Age of Jackson. For it was in 1833 that an American president for the first time proclaimed himself the "direct representative of the American people" and claimed to have been mandated by the people to do some particular deed for them while in office. This claim to a mandate, I mean to show, had real merit. Since that occasion, I further argue, the entanglement of the presidency with the American creed's preeminent value, democracy, has lost much of its meaningfulness. As a consequence, every president must now attempt to fulfill expectations that in the past were brought to bear against only exceptional administrations. The consequences are explored later in this chapter through a comparison of what it meant, in the administrations of Presidents Jackson and Kennedy, to make the anti-Madisonian boast "My president is a symbol of America's commitment to democracy." Before getting on with the comparison of the two men and their relationships with the public, however, I want to examine the word *democracy* itself, because the difference between Kennedy and Jackson as democratic icons, I think, reflects a radical change in the meaning of the term over a century and a half of American usage.

WHAT DEMOCRACY USED TO MEAN

In the 1800s, the word *democracy* had a threefold meaning. It referred not only to the process by which governmental decisions were made but also to the result achieved and to those who brought the result about. The democracy strove for democracy through democracy. *Democracy* thus denoted the operation in government of three principles: agency, purpose, and process. The first recorded American usage of the word *democracy* to refer to the popular class as the agents of democracy appeared in 1816, in congressional debate, but that usage was rare before the 1830s.[4] Thus in Noah Webster's *American Dictionary of the English Language*, published in 1828, *democracy* is defined simply as "government of the people; a form of government in which the supreme power is lodged in the hands of the people collectively, or in which the people exercise the power of legislation. Such was the government of Athens." Soon after Webster's dictionary went to press, however, events—described below—made his definition obsolete. For in the 1830s *democracy* (or *Democracy*, as followers of the Democratic party preferred to write) came to have, among its other meanings, the common people of the country.[5]

Democracy was also, from the 1830s through the early part of this century, the word used to describe the purpose for which the democracy struggled. As an end, democracy has historically implied a condition of equality. The legal equality of the citizens of the Greek demos was a central feature of Athenian democracy. When it was used to denote the ends of politics in America, *democracy* implied that the interest of common people in equality was to be advanced.

When Abraham Lincoln thus famously defined our form of government as one "of the people, by the people, for the people," he was not being redundant. He was, rather, delineating his century's understanding of democracy as a tripartite scheme.[6] Who were the agents of democracy? The people, the laboring classes, "the democracy," as opposed to "all the nice exclusive sort" that would stand in their way.[7] Even the famous plutocrat Andrew Carnegie spoke proudly of "the Democracy," which would soon triumph, he was certain, in his native Great Britain, as it had triumphed in his adopted land.[8] What was the purpose for which "the democracy" struggled? Again, democracy, understood by Democrats, Whigs, and Republicans alike as a condition of basic human equality. And how was the democracy to achieve democracy? Simple, through the democratic process, understood from before Lincoln's time to our own as enshrined in majoritarian rules and procedures. In Lincoln's restrained words: "Unanimity is impossible; the rule of a minority, as a permanent arrangement, is wholly inadmissible; so that, rejecting the majority principle, anarchy or despotism in some form is all that is left."[9] In the more enthusiastic words of Thomas Jefferson: "To consider the will of the society announced by the majority of a single vote, as sacred as if unanimous, is the first of all lessons in importance."[10]

WHAT DEMOCRACY MEANS TODAY

This complex understanding of *democracy* has been all but lost in this century, as the procedural meaning of the word has come to reflect its only widely accepted usage. The *Oxford American Dictionary*'s definition is consequently concise: "1. government by the whole people of a country, especially through representatives whom they elect. 2. a country governed in this way." The more loquacious *American Heritage Dictionary of the English Language* (3d ed.) includes: "3. the common people, considered as the primary source of political power." The latter dictionary is committed, as its name implies, to the preservation of the language, and I am unaware of any contemporary usage of the term to denote agency. *Democratic* is, of course, still used to mean the simple tastes of the common person and to designate a country in which there is a presumed equality of tastes. Social equality, however, is not the same as political or economic equality, a point to which I return in this chapter. In any event, when *democracy* is used to refer to a political objective today, its meaning is procedurally circumscribed. Modern democracy is a congeries of processes: public debates, media campaigns, hearings, appeals, demonstrations, and so on.

This is evident in the language chosen by the National Endowment for Democracy to explain itself. The endowment, a government-subsidized agency that promotes democracy around the globe, is a living embodiment of our country's understanding of democracy. In the endowment's report to Congress for the 1992 fiscal year, democracy is never precisely defined. It is, however, described as "a very complex system" that "must grow over time, sink roots, and earn legitimacy and loyalty." The chairman of the endowment further states in the report that

> democracy requires, among other elements:
> political parties that respond to the needs of citizens; trade unions that protect the rights of workers; a market economy that promotes an efficient exchange of goods and services; a civil society that spurs local participation; a free press that informs citizens; and an independent judiciary that respects the rule of law and safeguards human rights.[11]

This is a sensible listing of some procedural characteristics of the political system of the United States and other "free" countries. It suggests that democracy rests on communication and bargaining among agents in a pluralist political universe. Though rights and needs are mentioned, there is no suggestion as to how those might differ, if at all, from the processes used to determine them. What, then, happened to America's nineteenth-century understanding of democracy?

Though I can only venture a brief answer, it seems that the ideas of democratic agency and purpose were "done in" in this country by, respectively, the rise of the administrative state and the global expansion of America's interests. The administrative state, through its amelioration of the conditions of the poor and its cooptation of dissidence through interest-group representation and government payoffs, dissipated class conflict–which is what the battle of "the democracy" against its enemies was. In the administrative state, "the people" became a mass, as opposed to a class. The administrative revolution defanged populism and made the rhetoric of collective action safe for even conservatives to adopt. Thus, when Ronald Reagan, as president, reiterated the refrain "We the people," he was in no danger of inciting the popular classes against the rich. There is simply no counterpart in today's rhetoric to the enemies of the people conjured by political leaders from the premodern era (who assailed, in order, the "aristocracy," the "slavocracy," the "robber barons," and the "interests").

The fatal blow to "the democracy" was struck, according to Russell Hanson, the leading scholar of the term's changing American usage, in the New Deal's embrace of the values of capitalism. The New Deal's ideal of prosperity guaranteed by government activism, "of continuous and widespread consumption as the basic desideratum of social life," triumphed by winning the loyalties of the American working class.[12] In this way, despite Franklin Roosevelt's own flirtations with class conflict in 1936, the democracy lost its historical role. The government itself, composed not of representative members of the winning party, as in the Jacksonian spoils system, but of experts in the various branches of administrative science, would secure for workers their just portion of the social surplus. In the administrative state, citizens interact with the government as individual constituents or as members of an interest group. They seldom if ever have the opportunity to view themselves as part of a large aggregation of persons with a collective consciousness, such as "the democracy."

America's encounter with the world had a similar effect on the popular understanding of democracy as a goal to be sought in domestic politics. As in the case of freedom, discussed in Chapter Two, the possibility of embarrassment in the eyes of the world pressured American elites to rethink an important concept and its political implications. Only in this case, the pressure was to constrict, not expand, the scope of an idea. If America was to lead the world toward democracy, it would have to keep quiet its search for democracy at home.

Our modern streamlined view of democracy makes every president a democratic avatar. Since every president is elected by the people in their collective capacity, and since properly democratic procedures are the touchstone of democratic legitimacy, every modern president has the burden and opportunity of being the nation's spokesperson for democracy. Is it any wonder, then, that modern presidents sometimes seem unconstrained in claiming clairvoyance as to the interests and desires of the people? Is it any wonder that "we the people" so often respond with a stifled yawn or with millions of outstretched hands (palms up, in a begging posture)?

ANDREW JACKSON

Andrew Jackson was a most "democratical" president. His success in the presidency can be credited largely to his ability to reflect the values of an expanding electorate and to energize that electorate by assigning to the people a starring role in a titanic battle of the plain people against the "moneyed power." Jackson's success in mirroring the people's prejudices had significance, however, even beyond what was demonstrated in our analysis of the president's prophetic role. It served also as the foundation for Jackson's other lasting legacy: the elevation of democracy from a social norm to a political axiom.

The framers of the Constitution thought that the most democratic branch of government would be the House of Representatives. And until Andrew Jackson's presidency, their government worked, in this respect, according to plan. Of the period before General Jackson's administration, James Sterling Young writes that "no Jeffersonian President could come to cabinet meetings claiming public support or electoral mandates for *his* policy aims and views. Legislators might speak . . . with the authority of vox populi, but not Presidents."[13] When Andrew Jackson smashed the "Monster Bank" on behalf of the plain people of the country, he smashed alike the early republic's understanding of executive authority.

In his message accompanying the veto of the bank bill, Jackson not only declaimed in a new voice the American civil-religious narrative but also proclaimed the democratically instructed-delegate model of the presidency. The majority of the voters were to decide the issue of the bank's survival, and the president was to accept their instructions. "A general discussion will now take place," Jackson stated in his veto address, "eliciting new light and settling important principles; and a new Congress, elected in the midst of such discussion, and furnishing an equal representation of the people according to the last census, will bear to the capitol the verdict of public opinion, and, I doubt not, bring this important question to a satisfactory result."[14] As Jackson and his opponents both intended, the election of 1832 placed the bank issue at the forefront of the nationwide deliberations that were just beginning to characterize the election process. Following his victory, Jackson affirmed his mandate.

The president, Jackson announced, was the "direct representative of the American people" (*CMPP* 1309). The revolutionary nature of this boast was not lost on his contemporaries. As did many others, Henry Clay took aim at Jackson's assertion to have received instructions from public opinion as registered in this election. "I had supposed," said Clay,

> that the Constitution and the laws were the sole source of executive authority . . . that the issue of a presidential election was merely to place the Chief Magistrate in the post assigned to him. . . . But it seems that if, prior to an election, certain opinions, no matter how

> ambiguously put forth by a candidate, are known to the people, these loose opinions, in virtue of the election, incorporate themselves with the Constitution, and afterwards are to be regarded and expounded as parts of the instrument.[15]

Previous presidents, as Clay knew, had understood themselves to be the trustees of the people's interests, not the delegates of their preferences. If the people and the president differed, the president was to follow his conscience. The people could give their judgment of his actions at the next election. Jackson himself had endorsed the traditional conception of the president's position in the government, and his relationship to the people, in his 1830 annual message. In defending two pocket vetoes, Jackson stated on that occasion that he was heartened by the reflection that if he had erred in his judgment of the people's interests, the Constitution afforded "the means of soon redressing the error" by selecting someone else for his office at the next election (*CMPP* 1075). President Jackson sounded a similarly old-fashioned note in this message when he stated that, though he knew "of no tribunal to which a public man in this country" could appeal with more propriety "than the judgment of the people," in the discharge of his official duties he had no choice but to follow "the dictates of [his] own judgment" (*CMPP* 1074).

Jackson's subsequent assertion of a mandate was revolutionary because it was democratic. And it was democratic in the way that Americans of Jackson's time understood democracy. Jackson claimed to be leading the democracy to democracy through democracy. Each aspect of this claim can be analyzed separately. I begin, following Lincoln, with the Jacksonian innovation in establishing the presidency at the center of a government of the people.

"OF THE PEOPLE"

President Jackson was not shy about declaring himself the champion of only a subset of the population. "The Aristocracy and the Democracy of the country," proclaimed Jackson's New York supporters in one of their champion's campaigns, "are arrayed against each other."[16] Such a statement would seem out of place today, but in President Jackson's age, political leaders were clear about who their opponents were. Jackson warned the good people of the country against their foes in his farewell address. "The path of freedom," he reminded them, "is continually beset by enemies who often assume the disguise of friends" (*CMPP* 1526). "The men who profit" from the "paper-money system," from protective tariffs, and from other elements of the opposition program of governance have "struck their roots . . . deep in the soil" (*CMPP* 1525). It was not just the money power that was to be feared but the money*ed* power, for they, the rich, had "waged war upon the people." The result: "Whole cities and communities were oppressed, individuals impoverished and ruined" (*CMPP* 1522–23).

Knowing one's enemies makes it easier to recognize one's friends: "the agricultural, mechanical, and laboring classes of society," as well as small traders and what we would today call entrepreneurs (*CMPP* 1524). These proud people, Jackson continued in the same oration, were "the bone and sinew of the country—men who love[d] liberty and desire[d] nothing but equal rights and equal laws" (*CMPP* 1524). Recent scholarship confirms Jackson's depiction of his followers. Economically, they were not poor and not so dispossessed or oppressed as they apparently felt themselves to be. Nevertheless, they were the individualists and egalitarians of their day: free-market capitalists who reasoned that they could do better for themselves and their country if permitted to compete for their own advantages, without government subsidies or restraints.[17] Culturally and socially, they were, like their hero in the White House, more oriented toward the frontier than the settled urban establishments of the East, more Scots-Irish Presbyterian than Anglo-American Congregationalist or Episcopalian, more backcountry than tidal basin, more "ethnic" than "old stock."[18]

The class basis of the president's following was attested to in both the new party's platforms and its press. The *Democratic Review*, which began publication in 1837, was the party's official organ of opinion. In its first editorial, Jacksonianism's intellectual articulators sought to explain the meaning of their movement. "We have an abiding confidence," the *Review*'s editors wrote, "in the virtue, intelligence, and full capacity for self-government, of the great mass of our people—our industrious, honest, manly, intelligent millions of freemen." We stand against, the editorial continued, the antidemocratic governance of the "'better classes,'" which, once in power, surround themselves with wealth and splendor "at the expense of the producing mass."[19] In the party's platform of 1844, moreover, the trust of "the American Democracy" in "a clear reliance upon the intelligence, patriotism, and the discriminating justice of the American masses" was listed as the first principle of Democratic partisanship.[20]

In part, the Jacksonians put such faith in the common people because the civil religion of the country emphasizes their unique virtue. As George Bancroft, the leading intellectual associated with Jacksonianism, reasoned, free men freely debating and competing with one another are the natural and proper support of free government. Americans, Bancroft believed, "cannot agree in an absurdity; neither can they agree in a falsehood." As a consequence, that government that rests on reason will also rest on "the people and not on the few." "The spirit of God," Bancroft concluded, in a review of Jacksonianism, "breathes through the combined intelligence of the people."[21] The Jacksonians could also place such confidence in the democracy because their understanding of the people's status within government was complemented by a conception of the process whereby the people's interests could best be served. This process was government by the people.

"BY THE PEOPLE"

"We are opposed," the *Democratic Review* proclaimed, "to all self-styled 'wholesome restraints' on the free action of the popular opinion and will."[22] The Democrats therefore contrasted their plan for voter sovereignty with the view of government announced by Jackson's predecessor, John Quincy Adams. Adams held a complex view of government's responsibilities, which he articulated in his first annual message to Congress. We can learn much about the innovativeness of Jacksonian democracy by briefly studying this address of a leading anti-Jacksonian. To begin with, then, Adams held it to be axiomatic that "the nation blessed with the largest portion of liberty must in proportion to its numbers be the most powerful nation upon earth, and that the tenure of power by man is; in the moral purposes of his Creator, upon condition that it shall be exercised to ends of beneficence, to improve the condition of himself and his fellow-man" (*CMPP* 882). Though Jackson's supporters might have hesitated at the speaker's seeming enthusiasm for power, they too assumed that America's destiny was greatness and that all power should be used in a Godly manner. Nor would Jacksonians likely have differed over the next step in Adam's closely reasoned speech.

Some of the United States, Adams noted, had taken innovative actions on behalf of the people. "Can we," the president asked of his fellow officers of the national government, "fall behind our fellow-servants in the exercise of the trust committed to us for the benefit of our common sovereign by the accomplishment of works important to the whole?" (*CMPP* 882). The "common sovereign" to which Adams refers in this passage is not the ultimate Sovereign, God, but the one appropriately referred to with a lower case *s*, the people.

Where Adams took flight from common opinion, and where common opinion took offense at Adams, was in the president's next declaration: The government, its chief magistrate asserted, must not permit the people it serves to dictate the substance of that service. The people, supposedly sovereign, must be kept out of the governing process. "Were we to slumber in indolence," Adams warned, and announce to the world "that we are palsied by the will of our constituents, would it not be to cast away the bounties of providence?" (*CMPP* 882). In every Democratic party platform from 1844 to 1856, the Democrats' reliance on the common people was contrasted with "the creed and practice of Federalism, under whatever name or form, which [sought] to palsy the will of the constituent, and which conceive[d] no imposture too monstrous for popular credulity."[23]

The distinctiveness of the Jacksonian view may further be illustrated with reference to two practices of government and the meanings attributed to them: the presidential election and the president's use of his appointive powers. With reference to his election, President Jackson asserted that the people, by returning him to office, had settled the issue of the bank's demise:

> The case was argued to the people; and now that the people have sustained the President, notwithstanding the array of influence and power which was brought to bear upon him, it is too late, he confi-

> dently thinks, to say that the question has not been decided. Whatever may be the opinions of others [the president was addressing his cabinet], the President considers his reelection as a decision of the people against the bank. (*CMPP* 1226)

In the election of 1832, Jackson continued, he "was sustained by a just people," and he was now determined to "evince his gratitude by carrying into effect their decision so far as it depend[ed] upon him" (*CMPP* 1226).

Jackson's understanding of events made sense in light of innovations in campaigning made in 1832. A common complaint about presidential elections today is that candidates avoid straightforward and potentially polarizing positions. But in 1832, the electorate was clearly informed about and polarized in their opinions on the bank's survival. Jackson's opponents helped clarify the issue of the election by advertising Jackson's message vetoing the bank's recharter. Nicholas Biddle, the bank's president, thought the message so contemptible that he distributed thirty thousand copies of the document.[24] With more than two-thirds of the nation's newspapers echoing Biddle's and Clay's denunciations of the president, Jackson's supporters were under pressure to devise new ways to communicate to the people.[25] Fortunately for Jackson, they were up to the task. On at least one occasion, the president publicly pledged to "Take the Responsibility" for killing the Monster Bank, and his promise was reprinted in pro-Jackson pamphlets mailed by allied congressmen (at government expense) to their constituents. "Take the Responsibility" and other slogans were also hoisted on hickory poles in the ubiquitous campaign processions of that year.[26] The 1832 campaign was, moreover, the first occasion in American presidential history during which issue-related campaign items (buttons, ribbons, and the like) were widely distributed.[27]

The most important device that Jackson relied upon in making his election a mandate, however, was neither a hickory pole nor a pamphlet but the political party. The people who turned out in unprecedented numbers to support Jackson in 1828 and 1832 were the creators of the world's first mass party; their surge to the polls in 1828 and 1832 more than doubled the proportion of the eligible electorate which took part in presidential contests. As

Richard McCormick notes: "In 1824 there were only two states in which as many as fifty percent of the eligibles had voted; in 1832 eleven states exceeded that mark and in four of those–New Hampshire, New York, Kentucky, and Ohio–the turnout was over seventy percent."[28]

The difference between 1824 and the subsequent years was Jackson's effect on the organization of the political environment. In 1824's partyless race, five candidates vied for the people's vote. Jackson won the popular vote that year, and Adams the presidency, but the process itself failed to win the interest of the people. Jackson's claim in his subsequent elections to be fighting momentous battles on behalf of the common man excited common men to participate. When the elites who rose in opposition to Jackson and the Democracy began themselves to look to the people for support in presidential contests, the two-party system became firmly established throughout the electorate.[29]

The president's use of his appointive powers complemented his reliance upon party. Jackson was not the first president to replace an outgoing administration's officials with persons more to his own liking. That, after all, is what *Marbury v. Madison* was all about. Jackson removed no more than 20 percent of the total civil service during his two terms. Nevertheless, Jackson took the spoils system to new heights. In removing 252 executive officers, Jackson fired more men than his six predecessors combined.[30] What was most notable about the Jacksonian spoils sytem, however, was not the number of officials it affected but the principle it served.[31]

Postmaster General Amos Kendall was Jackson's principal adviser on appointments. He was also a theorist of patronage. He recognized that rotation in office according to partisanship would not only help to ensure a cadre of motivated followers for his political chief but would also free the government from dependence on the patrician class that had monopolized government work since the 1780s.[32] Thus Kendall routinized and coordinated the work of the Post Office. Before the Civil War, his innovations spread to the other government departments. Jacksonian reforms in administration were, in fact, extensive and included "functional specialization, executive staffs, a bureaucracy of linked offices within each agency, and efficiency records that marked officials on 'competence, faithfulness and attention.'"[33]

The practice of patronage came not to accord with its theory, and most nineteenth-century writers blamed Jackson for "setting in train the disastrous deterioration of American governmental service."[34] That Jackson's administrative innovations were not appreciated by the intellectual class of his century should not, however, obscure the point that it was through a principled yet practical partisan and administrative system that the Jacksonians strove to achieve their purpose, a government for the people.

"FOR THE PEOPLE"

"It is to be regretted," remarked President Jackson near the close of his first term, "that the rich and powerful too often bend the acts of government to their selfish purposes." Government aid to the rich is unjust, Jackson explained, because it disturbs the equality of opportunity to which every person is entitled. "The humble members of society–the farmers, mechanics, and laborers–who have neither the time nor the means" of securing government subsidies and favors have a right to be protected against this abuse of government. What should the government do, then, if not actively promote particular business concerns or, as we might say today, strategic trade sectors? "If it would confine itself to equal protection, and, as Heaven does its rains, shower its favors alike on the high and the low, the rich and the poor, it would be an unqualified blessing" (*CMPP* 1153).

The Jacksonians believed that equal protection under the laws would lead to a tolerably equal distribution of rewards to all. With the highborn cut down to size, America would be a fluid society with a permeable and ever-changing "ascendancy" of self-made men, like Jackson himself. The prevailing inequities in the distribution of wealth in the young nation, the Jacksonians believed, were the product of corruption. The most worrisome result of this corruption was the threat it posed to the virtues of the common people, who might stop striving fairly to gain what they saw others winning through unjust means. As Tocqueville, whose feelings about democracy were decidedly mixed, observed, in Jacksonian

America, the passion for equality was thus far and for the most part "manly and lawful," tending toward the elevation of "the humble to the rank of the great." America did not yet exhibit, Tocqueville was pleased to report, that contrasting and "depraved taste for equality, which impels the weak to attempt to lower the powerful."[35] The Jacksonians believed that their policies were necessary to prevent democracy from taking this much-feared descent into leveling.

Even Jackson's policy of forcibly removing Native Americans from areas of white settlement was an expression of his party's conception of the government's role in preserving a system of equal economic opportunity. Jackson and his supporters, argue Richard Ellis and Aaron Wildavsky, believed that only with the special help of the government would Native Americans be able to compete in the scramble for individual necessities and comforts. Better, then, that they be removed from the competition altogether, to lessen the need for government authority and controls.[36]

Democracy as the end of good government, finally, meant to the Jacksonians a fundamental equality in the respect owed to every member of society. Earlier in America, the "manly and lawful" refusal of the common people to bow and scrape before their betters had been popularly understood as an attribute of small-*r* republicanism. By the 1830s, however, republicanism had lost many of its affirmative associations, and its core concept of equality had come to be subsumed under the word *democracy.* Thus, for a prominent example, when Tocqueville wrote of American democracy, he meant, among other things, a basic equality in the respect that people in this country showed to one another. As *democracy* eclipsed *republicanism* as the word of choice to denote this aspect of equality, the last half of the Democratic-Republican's label became redundant and was eventually dropped.[37] Democracy, in the mid-nineteenth century, was a lexical as well as political hegemon.

THE PROGRESSIVE UNDERMINING OF DEMOCRACY

In his influential amendment to the thesis of a distinctly "modern" twentieth-century presidency, Jeffrey Tulis explored the innovative leadership of Presidents Theodore Roosevelt and Woodrow Wilson. In Tulis's understanding, modern presidents most differ from their predecessors in their reliance on popular speeches in which they enter into a direct relationship with the people. Tulis credits Theodore Roosevelt with first reaping the benefits of such an approach to office. Roosevelt pursued what he conceived of as conservative policies designed "to moderate disputes that [he] feared might anticipate and signal class antagonism severe enough to prompt civil war." In doing so, he distanced himself from his own party within Congress and took his message directly to the people.[38] Roosevelt stopped short, however, of attempts to arouse the public while Congress was actually deliberating on his proposals. Roosevelt thought of himself as *anti*demagogic. The nation, he believed, was in danger of being swept into chaos by demagoguery from the Left. The exceptional exercise of executive leadership was imperative to right the situation. His wish, Tulis notes, was that "his moderate statesmanship, more than his immoderate theory" (which set no clear bounds on an executive who perceived the nation to be at risk), would "be the precedent for future presidents" (115). In this, he was to be disappointed.

Wilson, as president and scholar, preached a radically personalized theory of the president's relationship with his public. Like many educated reformers of his time, he thought the Constitution was obsolete in an industrial age. Particularly at fault was the separation of powers, which, Wilson believed, limited the president's potential to lead the government along paths mandated by the electorate. On the one hand, Wilson's desire to make the American government more like the British parliamentary system promised to elevate the role of parties and the Congress as integral units in an invigorated government. On the other hand, Wilson's exaltation of leaders as men who divine the true sentiment of the people in an act of creative alchemy placed him increasingly at odds with his fellow partisans and made it almost inevitable that he would attempt to break free of their shackles once he perceived that their ability to interpret the public mind was not as keen as his own. In the aftermath of World War I, Wilson abandoned the constraints implicit in his theory of statesmanship and took to a new extreme Theodore Roosevelt's claim to be bound personally to the people in a promissory relationship.

Jackson also made and kept promises to the people. But his promises were influenced by his and the people's appreciation of the role of other institutions within government–especially the parties and Congress. Nineteenth-century presidents generally were reluctant to claim an unmediated relationship with the people, even when they felt they and their party were mandated by election to pursue particular goals. Presidents of the prior century, even after the democratization of the presidential selection process in the 1830s, simply did not think it proper *personally* to present their views on policy before the public. It is, in this light, no coincidence that Jackson's revolution in governance occurred in the pursuit of *re*election. As the historian M. J. Heale has written, President, as opposed to candidate, Jackson, "by carrying out his public duties with belligerent devotion . . . could associate himself with causes without resorting to the kind of electioneering which had always been reprobated."[39] The fact that presidents and would-be presidents alike viewed personal appeals to the people as beneath the dignity of the office that George Washington once held worked to preserve the integrity of the parties and the deliberative role of the Congress. Presidential nominees, in the era of strong party competition, were, one historian has written, "political symbols to be bent to the party's will."[40] They might grow once in office, as did Jackson, but for the most part, presidents from the 1820s to the 1890s did not claim a greatness that was not theirs.

With the gradual acceptance of Wilson's vision, the constitutional balance preserved, if transformed, in Jackson's revolution was undone. The results for the understanding of the presidency as a democratic institution were several. The collapse of the party system under the weight of the exalted presidency undermined the institutional foundation of democratic agency. If the democracy of plain people was no longer embodied in the Democracy, or in

Populist or populist-Republican campaigns such as that of 1840, how could common folk maintain their collective political identity? Democratic agency was further undermined by the policies pursued by Roosevelt and Wilson, which weakened class antagonisms and hence blurred the distinction between the democracy and the rest of the population.

Progressive successes in electoral reform proved particularly important in marginalizing the democracy's traditional demands for a rough economic equality. This was a bitter irony to Herbert Croly and other Progressive leaders, who had hoped early in the century that energetic presidential leadership would rally the democracy in its pursuit of the "economic, social, and moral emancipation" of the people against "those obstacles which the economic development of the country ha[d] placed in the path of a better democratic fulfillment."[41] "There is no glory," thought the more radical Progressives, "in standing for the principles of political democracy."[42] Glorious or not, political democracy, understood as woman's suffrage, the primary, the referendum, and then civil rights, began early in this century to eclipse older concerns of economic redistribution. The result: Americans have a deep-seated belief that theirs is the most democratic society in the world, quite simply regardless of disparities in wealth and power. This, as Gordon Wood points out (seemingly without appreciating its irony), is "equality as no other nation has ever quite had it."[43]

As agency and purpose were squeezed out of the definition of *democracy*, the term's procedural aspect thus came ever more to the fore. A president claiming a democratic mandate would no longer be judged critically. A democratic leader was not one who represented the democracy in its struggle for democracy through democracy. Now, a democratic leader was simply one who held the office whose occupant was normally elected in a choice of all the people. The president, by simple virtue of his position in office, could now claim to be the personally delegated champion of the entire nation. Once the executive, in the 1930s and 1940s, accepted new responsibilities for the public's welfare, the presidency grew even larger in the public's consciousness. Before Franklin Roosevelt's administration, a president might choose *not* to claim the role of the people's personal champion. One might consult, for example, the record of the Taft administration.[44] After Franklin Roosevelt, however, no president could escape the shadow of his progressive predecessors.[45]

This, briefly, is how American democracy lost its voice. When it lost its voice, it lost also its ability to discriminate between the exceptional and the commonplace executive. I pursue this argument below in an examination of the relationship between the people and John F. Kennedy.

JOHN F. KENNEDY

"*JFK* completes the journey from fact to fantasy," Edward Epstein wrote in the *Atlantic Monthly*.[46] Epstein's subject was Oliver Stone's brazenly fictionalized film about the president's assassination. His subject might well have been the late president's administration itself. It should come as no surprise, in fact, that Kennedy's death has been the object of the fevered imaginations of directors, writers, journalists, and conspiracy buffs, for the man's entire presidency was built around a Hollywood persona that bore a tantalizing but superficial relation to reality.

The manufacturing of the Kennedy legend is itself now legendary. Even casual observers of politics (or is it culture?) know how Joseph Kennedy Sr. bought his way into the service of Franklin Roosevelt; how the father's ambitions for his family came to rest on "Jack's" shoulders after the death of his more gifted older brother; how the younger son's disastrous handling of a navy torpedo boat was ignored while his subsequent heroism was exaggerated; how, as a young congressman, Kennedy won a Pulitzer Prize for a book he probably did not write; and how the president, who had personally overseen the creation of the Green Berets and had greatly expanded America's military presence in Vietnam, was reported by his sycophantic admirers to have been on the very verge of withdrawing the troops from Vietnam when he was killed in Dallas. Perhaps the most revealing aspect of the Kennedy legend, however, was the president's "imprisonment" by sex.[47]

The American head of state, given the personalism and intimacy of his relationship with the people, can hardly escape entanglement in something so human and elemental as sex. Certainly Kennedy did not. From the time he entered the contest for the presidency, Kennedy was (and apparently remains) the object of his admirers' fantasies. Thus, though the prurient interest that Kennedy took in a great many of the women surrounding him was only fully known at the time by those closest to him, it was repaid many times over by his adoring fans. John F. Kennedy, in the language of Madison Avenue, had sex appeal.

He was, author Garry Wills believes, the beneficiary in this respect of the *first* post–World War II sexual revolution. The literary, artistic, and societal assault upon conventional mores which took place in the late 1950s was only an ironic precursor to the later revolution in women's roles and expectations. "It is hard to remember," Wills writes, "that the 'sexual revolutionaries' of the 1950s–male *and* female–had been brought up on the cult of Hemingway, of dominating men, hunters, bull-fighters, risk-takers" (28). Norman Mailer, a Hemingway wanna-be himself, wrote a campaign piece for *Esquire* which the author claimed to have won the election for Kennedy. In that article, Mailer asserted that in America, a hero was one who "could fight well, kill well (if always with honor), love well and love many, be cool, be daring, be dashing, be wild, be wily, be resourceful, be a brave gun." Woman's role was to be among the "many" getting "loved well."[48] And love many he did, including Judith Campbell, the mistress of Sam Giancana, a gangster from Chicago whom the CIA asked for help in its attempt to kill Fidel Castro.[49]

Kennedy's reckless assignations with a mobster's moll were not publicly known while he lived. What the public knew during the campaign and the presidency was that a dashing young man from a wealthy family, married to a stunningly attractive woman, was being paraded around the country as a celebrity. Like a celebrity, Gil Troy writes of Kennedy in 1960, he "was famous, it seemed, simply for being famous. His campaign literature illustrated the circularity of this approach, stressing his 'unique voter appeal,' his 'nationwide profile and fame,' his status as a 'Top Television and Platform Personality.'"[50] Fittingly, the theme song of the Kennedy campaign, "High Hopes," was adapted from a show tune popularized in an otherwise forgettable Hollywood film. The lyrics epitomized the circularity Troy found in Kennedy's campaign literature:

Everyone is voting for Jack
'Cause he's got what all the rest lack,
Everyone wants to back Jack,
Jack is on the right track.

'Cause he's got high hopes,"[51]

What the public did not know, however, they could imagine, and the vicarious thrills that the people could take in giving themselves to Kennedy went beyond the mere enjoyment of the exercise of power analyzed in Chapter Three.

The president, it seems, is our property now, and we will do with him as we please. If he is clumsy, like Ford, we will make a national pastime of recording his mishaps; if he is sanctimonious, like Carter, we will mock (and test) his faith; if he is private, like Nixon, we will demand to know his secrets; and if he is romantic, like Kennedy, we will imagine ourselves the subjects of his happy kingdom.[52] Whatever the president is, that is what he stands for. If a president actually comes into office in a campaign that focuses at least indirectly on issues, very well. Like Reagan in his first term, he will have an opportunity to pursue a policy revolution. But most presidents, now as well as in the past, are more like Kennedy than Reagan, more like Chester Arthur than Franklin Roosevelt. In the past, an unexceptional man might hide out in the White House for four years. That is no longer a possibility.

Kennedy was elected by only a bare plurality. In his campaign, he had promised to have high hopes and to get the nation moving again. Nevertheless, Kennedy had no choice but to claim a mandate once he entered office. But what could his mandate be? Kennedy's elite backers, the policymakers and opinion leaders, had some ideas. Kennedy had won the election, they believed, so that he might offer bold new ideas in domestic policy and increase America's resolve to win the Cold War. But Kennedy's popular mandate was not so much an answer to the question, Where are we being led? but How? The answer: with that celebrated Kennedy style; with freneticism, courage in the face of long odds, and vigor. As Bruce Miroff has argued, the Kennedy style may have lacked substance, but it was not without consequence. It led Kennedy to treat episodes of conflict as opportunities to demonstrate his celebrated courage and machismo. This habit of thought, Miroff contends, helped to land us in a major war in Vietnam.[53]

Who exactly was the president leading? Not the democracy; that usage had dropped into obscurity well before the 1960s. And for what purpose was vigor to be expended? Not for democracy, at least not for democracy at home. The American encounter with the world which began at the turn of the century made Americans defensive about their society. How could we make the world safe for that which we still fought for at home? In the tense Cold War atmosphere of the Kennedy administration, which the president and the people exacerbated with his and their desire to demonstrate toughness, it was taken for granted that democracy as an end had been all but perfected in America.

A JACKSON COUNTERPOINT: THE PEGGY EATON AFFAIR

Before bringing this chapter to a close, it is worthwhile to journey once more to the 1820s and 1830s, for the contrast between the relationship of the people with President Kennedy and their relationship with President Jackson is more precise than most people today probably realize. Jackson's administration was also deeply "sexualized." The most important event of the latter half of Jackson's administration was of course the war against the bank and all that involved. But to observers at the time, the most noteworthy event of the first several years of the Jackson presidency was probably the Peggy Eaton affair.

Peggy Eaton was the wife of Andrew Jackson's first secretary of war, John Eaton, a fellow Tennesseean and a member of the Senate when Jackson chose him for his cabinet. The Eatons had been married, at the urging of the president-elect, just three months before Jackson's inauguration and less than a year after the death of Peggy's first husband. The Eatons had been in haste because they had been lovers, it seems, for some time. It is said, in fact, that when Peggy's first husband, John Timberlake, died in 1828 aboard the frigate *Constitution*, he thereby "relinquish[ed] the employment Senator John Eaton had obtained for him by posting a bond in the sum of ten thousand dollars to insure an improvement in the purser's accounting."[54] The president-elect thought that the marriage would forestall any trouble from the appointment of the groom to his cabinet. Jackson was mistaken. The wives of Jackson's other cabinet members, as well as Emily Donelson, hostess in the widower's White House, refused to call upon the new Mrs. Eaton.

Jackson's own late wife, Rachel, had similarly been married to another man when she and Andrew Jackson first cohabited. In Jackson's case, there had been an honest misunderstanding. Rachel's first husband had told her that their divorce had been filed with the proper authorities. When this proved not to be the case, the embarrassed bigamist and her adulterous husband hurriedly secured the divorce decree and then remarried. These details were widely known at the time, and despite Jackson's willingness (which he demonstrated in 1806) to kill any man who insulted his wife, the Jacksons suffered numerous slanders. When his wife died shortly after the 1828 election, Jackson was certain that it was out of grief for having been mistreated during his campaign. Perhaps because of his memories of his own wife's rumor-scarred life, Jackson was steadfast in defense of his "little friend Peg."[55]

When two clergymen criticized the Eatons, Jackson convened a cabinet meeting to address their accusations. When the clergymen admitted that they had no eyewitness testimony to prove that Mrs. Eaton was a woman of loose morals, Jackson exploded with his own finding. "She is chaste as a virgin!" exclaimed the president.[56] Political intrigue followed, as Martin Van Buren adroitly exploited the tensions that the affair had created within the cabinet. The result was an administration shake-up that drove the anti-Peg and anti-Jacksonian Calhoun out of the vice presidency and positioned Van Buren as the heir apparent.

What can we make of this affair, which was relayed across the nation in the partisan newspapers of that time? President Jackson's defense of Peggy Eaton was surely motivated by his personal feelings. But his actions were of public significance. In upholding the honor of Mrs. Eaton—the daughter of an innkeeper and the former wife of a sailor–Jackson upheld the dignity of the common people of America. It was the haute monde, as Marquis James, the most thorough chronicler of the affair, notes, that was aghast at Mrs. Timberlake-Eaton. It was the more democratic Mr. Van Buren (who also benefited in this instance from his bachelor status) who came to her defense within the cabinet (509). It was the democracy (and the Democracy's newspaper, the *Globe*), whose more tolerant views of such things were defended by the president. Even in his White House's envelopment by sex, then, Jackson was a symbol for his age. Where Kennedy was secretive, Jackson was open; where Kennedy pursued uncommon women, Jackson defended the reputation of a common man and woman and thereby upheld the dignity of all the plain people who could sympathize with the Eatons as victims of the better sort's duplicitous prudery.

CONCLUSION

Old-style democracy was like a prism. It took the light emanating from a president's claim to be a symbol of democracy and refracted it into three bands, each with its own properties. A nineteenth-century president could thus be subjected to an impressive range of questions about his "democraticness." Was the president *of* the democracy? Was he a fit representative of the bone and sinew of the American laboring classes? Was the president elected *by* democracy? Did he come into office at the head of an organization that granted the power of decision to the people? Finally, was the president *for* democracy? Was he pursuing democratic equality?

New-style democracy, by contrast, is like a fun-house mirror. It entertains by making everyone look equally ridiculous. By the lights of our contemporary understanding of democracy, every president (save the never-elected Gerald Ford) appears thoroughly democratic. Was the president elected in a public ritual granting the power of final decision to a plurality of voters? If he rose from the vice presidency, was he elected to that office in the same national elections? Very well, then; the president is a fit symbol of our commitment to democracy. He is Our Man in Washington; our national spokesman; our property.

5

THE PEOPLE RESPOND TO PRESIDENTIAL PREROGATIVE

WHEN A PRESIDENT RESPONDS TO A CRISIS BY ACTING for the public good when the law is silent, or even against the law, he exercises a particular type of power, which is called prerogative.[1] In a sense, everyone possesses prerogative power. Were you to scale your neighbor's fence to save a child from drowning, you would rely upon the good sense of the local prosecutor not to try you for trespass. In a similar example from John Locke's *Second Treatise*, a man "pulls down an innocent man's house when the next to is burning." By so doing, he "comes within the reach of the law." But it would be wrong, Locke argues, to uphold the letter of the law in such an instance, for "the laws themselves should in some cases give way to . . . this fundamental law of nature and government, viz. That as much as may be, all the members of the society are to be preserved" (ibid.). The executive, then, is hardly unique in possessing prerogative power. Because of the constitutional attributes of his office, however, he is more likely to have recourse to this power than are most persons, including most other government leaders.[2]

Because his base of support is national and independent from the Congress and because he shares his office with no one, the president can act with decisiveness, energy, and secrecy. These, the Constitution's framers knew, were fit attributes for a leader who would take responsibility in times of crisis.[3] But if prerogative is seemingly unavoidable, it is also clearly in conflict with the democratic creed that legitimates our government. What, if any, boundaries are there, then, to executive prerogative? Is it nonsense even to ask that question, given prerogative's meaning?

In seeking to answer these questions–to determine what rules, if any, guide the presidential exercise of prerogative and the public's response to it–I begin by disposing of the argument that precise boundaries are to be found in law. The fate before the courts of good Samaritans who "take the law into their own hands" has varied from case to case. A brief review of some leading Supreme Court cases will demonstrate that this is as true of presidents as of anyone else.

THE SUPREME COURT EXAMINES PREROGATIVE

At the outset of the Civil War, Abraham Lincoln ordered a blockade of southern ports. When the Congress came into special session three months later, it sought retroactively to authorize the president's decision. Shipowners whose property had been seized in the meantime brought suit against the government. The plaintiffs claimed that the president, in having ordered a blockade in the first place, had usurped Congress's sole authority to declare war. Speaking for a majority of the justices, Justice Grier observed in *The Prize Cases* that the war, having "sprung forth suddenly from the parent brain, a Minerva in the full panoply of war," had presented Lincoln with no choice but to act. "The President," Justice Grier concluded, "was bound to meet [the war] in the shape it presented itself, without waiting for Congress to baptize it with a name."[4] In further Civil War–era cases, the Court upheld other extraordinary presidential acts, including Lincoln's suspensions of the writ of habeas corpus.[5]

After the war, and after the crisis leader's death, the Court expressed second thoughts and "enlisted," as Arthur Schlesinger Jr. wrote, "in the effort to bridle the Presidency."[6] In *Ex Parte Milligan*, a citizen of Indiana who had been sentenced by a military commission to be hanged petitioned for a writ of habeas corpus. Such petitions had been routinely denied at the executive's discretion during the war. The Court, reversing its decision in a prior case, granted the petition and declared that for the executive to suspend a citizen's right and subject him to military rule in an area where the regular courts were functioning was a "pernicious" and "false" doctrine leading "directly to anarchy or despotism."[7]

In the crisis presidency of Franklin Roosevelt, the Court similarly changed course once the emergency had passed. At the close of Roosevelt's first term, executives of the Curtiss-Wright Export Corporation sought to reverse their convictions for having violated a presidentially ordered arms embargo. The plaintiffs in the appeal argued that Congress, in granting the president authority to embargo arms to South America, where Bolivia and Paraguay were at war, had unconstitutionally delegated its powers to the executive. Ranging far afield from the particular controversy before the Court, Justice Sutherland, speaking for a near-unanimous majority, declared that the president possesses inherent and exclusive powers to promote the interests of the nation. The president, stated Justice Sutherland, has a "plenary and exclusive power" in foreign affairs.[8] The *Curtiss-Wright* holding has been subjected to damning criticism by legal scholars. Nevertheless, it continues to be cited with conviction by executive-branch attorneys and presidential agents (including, for a recent example, Lieutenant Colonel Oliver North).[9]

During World War II, the Court continued in the direction indicated in *Curtiss-Wright.* In a number of cases, the Court gave its imprimatur to the president's assumption of unusual powers. The most notorious such case was *Korematsu v. United States,* in which the Court upheld the president's order relocating West Coast American residents of Japanese ancestry to detention camps in the interior of the country. Only after the war was won, and after the death of the crisis leader, did the Court again speak "the language of limitation."[10] It did so in *Duncan v. Kahanamoku,* a case similar to the post–Civil War decision reviewed previously. In *Duncan,* the Court declared unconstitutional the president's imposition of martial law in Hawaii, singling out the suspension of the writ of habeas corpus as a particularly egregious act. As for the president's alleged inherent power to decide for himself when an otherwise illegal act is rightful: "Executive action is not proof of its own necessity" (167). The difference in the Court's findings, as Edward Corwin observed some time ago, is "quite simply explicable. When the Korematsu case was decided the war was still waging; when the Hawaiian Martial Law cases were decided, fighting had ceased."[11]

The pattern was repeated, finally, in the presidency of Roosevelt's successor, Harry Truman. Although the way in which Truman had taken the nation to war in Korea raised a host of constitutional questions, the Court did not have an occasion to voice an opinion on any of them until the war was virtually won. On April 8, 1952, one day before a nationwide walkout in the steel industry was to take effect, Harry Truman ordered his commerce secretary to seize and operate the nation's steel mills. Truman's Wage Stabilization Board had recommended a pay increase for the workers, but the companies refused to go along unless they were permitted a hefty hike in the price of steel. Truman, according to biographer David McCullough, "considered the industry's proposed price increase little better than profiteering."[12] Declaring in a nationwide address that the steel companies were "recklessly forcing a shutdown" that would imperil the national defense, Truman declared it his "plain duty" to prevent a stoppage in steel production.[13]

As Truman saw it, "A little reading of history would have shown that there was nothing unusual about this action."[14] "The President has the power," Truman told his staff, "to keep the country from going to hell." If that meant taking over the steel mills, so be it. And if a president, Truman was asked at a press conference, determined that it was necessary to order the seizure of the newspapers and radio stations, could he do that too? "Under similar circumstances, the President of the United States has to act for whatever is best for the country," he replied.[15]

What Truman had neglected was the timing of his action. As Robert Hirschfield noted, by the time the steel seizure case was decided, "truce talks had long been under way in Korea and the emergency seemed to have passed its most critical stage."[16] The seizure was not necessary to win the war in Korea. In his public statements at the time, and in his memoirs, Truman implicitly acknowledged this. He defended his action with reference not so much to Korea as to the widening Cold War. "Any failure on our part to deliver what we had promised to furnish our allies under the Mutual Defense Assistance Program would seriously undermine their faith in our ability to aid them in critical moments," Truman wrote. "Russia," Truman continued, "would be cheered" by the strike, seeing in it "evidence of a slowdown in our rearmament." Russia's cheer might lead, Truman had concluded in consultation with his secretary of state, Dean Acheson, to "other 'Koreas.'"[17] This chain of reasoning led further and further from the immediate threat to American lives in Korea. The fact that Truman had acted before exhausting available statutory authority to deal with the threatened shutdown also cast doubt on the necessity of the president's recourse to prerogative. The Taft-Hartley Law, originally vetoed by Truman, authorized the president to seek a court injunction for a sixty-day "cooling off" period during which workers in a critical industry would be barred from striking. Further steps, involving both the executive and Congress, would be set in motion once the court issued an injunction. Union leaders and liberal Democrats had opposed Taft-Hartley, and Truman was loath to proceed under its mantle.[18] Nevertheless, the act well expressed the will of the people in Dwight Eisenhower's election year.

In declaring Truman's seizure unconstitutional, the Court drew back from the inherent-powers theory it had upheld in *Curtiss-Wright.* But the Court did not in any sense resolve the issue of presidential prerogative. Indeed, as if to underscore the fundamental ambiguity of this area of law, each of the six justices in the majority issued his own opinion explaining the verdict.[19]

Just because prerogative has not been clearly defined by the Supreme Court does not mean, however, that there are no rules to be discerned from the history of prerogative acts. The limits to prerogative are in our thoughts rather than our laws. The story to be told regarding prerogative thus recalls elements of that told in Chapters One and Three. As with their ideas about civil religion and charisma, the people, unlike the Court, have been fairly constant in their thinking about prerogative. Presidential prerogative has been judged by a consistently pragmatic standard: Was the president's exercise of unusual powers necessary; was it intended for the public's benefit? This is a single, not a dual, standard, for the public's estimate of necessity has been tied to its estimate of presidential intent. When Lincoln ordered a blockade of southern ports, it was clear to all parties why he had done so. When Truman ordered the seizure of the nation's steel mills, his motivation was not above question. The head of the Inland Steel Company accused the president on nationwide television of seizing the mills to pay a political debt to the Congress of Industrial Organizations (CIO). Senator Robert Taft, coauthor of the law that the president had bypassed in his apparent haste to assert personal control over the dispute, called for the president's impeachment.[20]

In assessing a president's intention, furthermore, the public seems guided by the character of the president. "Great men" are permitted great acts; lesser men–whose concern is not unquestionably for the public but rather for themselves–are held more closely to the letter of the law. Locke understood perfectly: "They have a very wrong notion of government, who say, that the people have encroached upon the prerogative, when they have got any part of it to be defined by positive laws. For in so doing, they have not pulled from the Prince any thing, that of right belonged to him, but only declared, that that power which they indefinitely left in his, or his ancestors', hands, to be exercised for their good, was not a thing, which they intended him, when he used it otherwise."[21]

Before elaborating on this theme, a question arises. What of presidents such as George Bush? Bush was not manifestly a "great man," a "God-like Prince," to use Locke's words for an executive to whom the people most readily defer. Yet he took the nation to war, relying largely on the president's alleged prerogative unilaterally to define and promote the nation's interests abroad.

PREROGATIVE POWER AND THE LESS-THAN-GREAT PRESIDENT

On August 1, 1990, George Bush learned that Iraq had invaded Kuwait. The next day, the president froze Iraqi assets in the United States. By August 8, Bush had ordered 250,000 troops to the area. Less than two months later, the president doubled the U.S. deployment, though he declined to announce the fact to the public until one week later. Congress temporized by holding hearings. Eventually, Bush invited Congress to join up. But first, the president secretly approved a war plan to reclaim occupied Kuwait, won the support of the United Nations, and negotiated the participation in the planned use of force of some twenty-seven other countries. Bush's invitation to Congress, sent by letter on January 8, was acted upon positively on January 12. Four days later the war began, right on the president's schedule. Had Congress not consented, Bush made it clear at the time, he would not have been deterred.[22]

George Bush was not supposed to have such power. Congress, in the waning stages of the Vietnam War, had passed the War Powers Resolution over Richard Nixon's veto. The resolution requires a president to consult with Congress "in every possible instance" before sending troops into imminent hostilities. The resolution requires further that "in the absence of a declaration of war," the president shall submit to Congress within forty-eight hours of any such deployment a report to Congress setting forth the rationale and legal grounds for his actions. If, within sixty days of the filing of this report, Congress neither declares war nor extends the deadline, the president "shall terminate any use of United States Armed Forces with respect to which such report was submitted (or required to be submitted)."[23] The War Powers Resolution was flawed legislation. It granted the president carte blanche to use the armed forces for military engagements lasting fewer than sixty days, and it was silent about how the sixty-day clock might be set ticking absent a presidential report to the Congress. Most fundamentally, the War Powers Resolution was based on a false premise: that precise legal boundaries could be established to define the limits of prerogative.

In addition to demonstrating the irrelevance of the War Powers Resolution, there were four other irritating features to the Persian Gulf War. First, the American ambassador to Iraq had unwittingly emboldened Saddam Hussein when she told him only days before the conquest that the United States took no position on "Arab-Arab conflicts," including Iraq's border dispute with Kuwait.[24] Second, Iraq might not have had the military capability to launch its invasion without the military assistance provided it during the 1980s by the United States. Third, the war restored sovereignty to Kuwait but terminated neither the regime nor the life of Saddam Hussein, who, after the disaster to the south of his country, turned his attention to the killing of Kurds in the north. Fourth, and finally, the war, proclaimed by Bush to be a holy war in the American civil-religious tradition, was in truth guided by balance-of-power considerations and by the Western nations' and Japan's dependence on Middle Eastern oil. Despite these flaws in the buildup to, the execution of, and the justification for this war, the president was arguably pursuing the nation's interests by leading us into hostilities, and the military outcome was decisive. The war was also relatively cost-free in terms of American casualties–148 Americans died in battle, 35 from "friendly fire."[25] All the dead were, furthermore, volunteers, the draft having ended in 1973.

Operation Desert Storm was not the great act of a great president. It was, however, tolerable from a pragmatic point of view. In a passage noted briefly in Chapter Three, John Locke again makes our point well: "For the people," Locke writes, "are very seldom, or never scrupulous, or nice in the point: they are far from examining prerogative, whilst it is in any tolerable degree employed for the use it was meant; that is, for the good of the people, and not manifestly against it."[26] The people do not, as is widely believed, necessarily rally around the president whenever he invokes their patriotism. When the public's support of the president does increase in times of trial, furthermore, that extra support is often fleeting. As George Edwards observes: "The famous 5 percentage point increase in approval accorded President Kennedy immediately following the invasion of Cuba at the Bay of Pigs was succeeded by a 6 percentage point decline in the next poll–despite the public's pride in the first manned U.S. space flight."[27] What the Gulf War example suggests, however, is that the public looks magnanimously upon presidential acts arguably taken on their behalf by a less-than-great president.

Magnanimity is a "a nobility of feeling; superiority to petty resentment or jealousy; generous disregard of injuries."[28] It is a virtue expected of royalty. That it is a virtue demonstrated by the people in their judgment of presidents would not, I think, have surprised our government's founders. As Gouverneur Morris said of the Constitution's design for an executive: "This Magistrate is not the King, but the prime-minister. The people are the King."[29] The people's magnanimity will suffice when the president sends troops into a minor military engagement. Sometimes, however, the presidency is occupied by a man more truly compelled by necessity than was George Bush to transgress more fully the bounds of ordinary law. On such occasions, the president assumes the by-now familiar stance of the sovereign, and the people look with deference upon their maximum leader.

The distance between magnanimity and deference is the distance between George Bush on the one hand and Thomas Jefferson, Abraham Lincoln, and Franklin Roosevelt on the other. The last three, notable for their assertions of prerogative, offered quite distinct justifications for their acts. Their arguments really did not matter. All three were great men, and in the presidency, great men dare as they please.

THREE PRESIDENTS IN THE TAKE-CHARGE TRADITION

Periodically, scholars of the presidency have been asked to rank the subjects of their studies. In each of six polls, beginning with Arthur Schlesinger Sr.'s 1948 survey, the experts have ranked Abraham Lincoln first, Franklin Roosevelt either second or third (behind or ahead of George Washington), and Thomas Jefferson either fourth or fifth. Other great or near-great presidents have included Woodrow Wilson, Andrew Jackson, Theodore Roosevelt, and James Polk.[30] All were presidents whose most famous acts in office were achieved through the exercise of prerogative power.

George Washington, in his pursuit of strict neutrality and non-entanglement, claimed for the president the right to speak exclusively for the nation in foreign affairs. Thomas Jefferson's most famous and momentous act as president, discussed later, was the purchase of Louisiana. Jefferson made it even though he believed the purchase had no basis in the Constitution. Andrew Jackson fought vigorously for powers that we now casually accept as the president's by right. James Polk usurped the war powers of the Congress by provoking Mexico into war. Abraham Lincoln took numerous extraconstitutional acts, including the embargo of southern ports and the suspension of the writ of habeas corpus, mentioned above and discussed more fully below. Theodore Roosevelt, as he boasted in his autobiography, "took Panama." And when he detected a "very, very slight undertone of veiled truculence" in the Japanese attitude toward the United States, he sent the battle fleet halfway around the world to overawe Japan's leadership and dared the Congress not to appropriate funds for its return.[31] Woodrow Wilson led the government in an extraordinary suppression of individual rights during World War I, while the second President Roosevelt, finally, took the nation to war twice—once at home in the New Deal and once abroad. In both instances, he exercised powers nowhere to be found in the executive article of the Constitution.

To be trusted with the tremendous powers wielded by these men is not the president's right. It has on occasion been the president's opportunity. Those who took the opportunity to exercise prerogative and got away with it exclusively constitute the presidential pantheon.

THOMAS JEFFERSON

In assuming the presidency in 1801, Jefferson and his supporters styled his election a "Revolution."[32] It was, to be more precise, intended as a restoration. Jefferson believed, that is, that the nation he had fought to establish was being subverted from within by objective allies of the British crown. Necessity compelled urgent action to return the country to the path of virtue. The purchase of Louisiana from France was one of those urgent actions.

The addition of Louisiana doubled the territory of the nation, ensured the loyalty to the United States of its western inhabitants, and permitted the United States to maintain—if temporarily—its distance from the warring powers of Europe. Jefferson also believed that the bargain he struck with Napoleon would allow the United States to ward off urbanization "for a thousand years."[33] And since cities, Jefferson thought, added "just so much to the support of pure government as sores do to the strength of the human body," Jefferson was persuaded that only an agrarian America could maintain its liberty. Those who worked the earth, Jefferson asserted, were "the most virtuous and independent citizens," the "chosen people of God," "whose breasts he has made his peculiar deposit for substantial and genuine virtue."[34]

It requires a bit of imagination to apprehend some of the interests Jefferson believed were staked to the Louisiana Purchase. To understand why the purchase troubled Jefferson's conscience requires even more. To a modern reader, it may seem self-evident that the United States had a right to expand its territory and to incorporate into the United States such new territories as it had acquired. Thomas Jefferson disagreed.

As a "strict constructionist," Jefferson felt strongly that government had the powers specifically deeded to it by the Constitution and no more. Constitutionalism, Henry Adams observed, was "the breath of his political life."[35] "The general government has no powers but such as the constitution has given it," to use Jefferson's words, "and it has not given it a power of holding foreign territory, and still less of incorporating it into the Union."[36] Therefore, Jefferson wrote, "I think it will be safer not to permit the enlargement of the Union but by amendment of the Constitution."[37] Jefferson, before he allowed himself to be persuaded to put constitutional scruples aside, thus drew up a draft amendment sanctioning the purchase. He did not agree to put the amendment (and his scruples) aside easily.

In the summer before Congress convened in special session to debate the purchase, Jefferson anxiously considered and reconsidered his position. "The Executive," Jefferson acknowledged in a letter penned in August, "in seizing the fugitive occurrence which so much advances the good of their country, have done an act beyond the Constitution." Soon, the Senate must be asked to ratify the treaty. The House must stand ready to appropriate the funds promised therein. Once these acts are done, Jefferson wrote, the Congress should "throw themselves on their country for doing for them unauthorized, what we know they would have done for themselves had they been in a position to do it."[38] Jefferson still had in mind at this time a constitutional amendment. In throwing themselves before the people, the Congress would ask for absolution in a formal alteration of the Constitution. But by early September, Napoleon seemed to be having second thoughts, and the situation became urgent.

Wilson Cary Nicholas, senator from Virginia, joined what was by then a chorus of advisers urging Jefferson to accept a broad construction of the Constitution. If construed liberally, Jefferson's supporters insisted, the nation's founding document might be found to sanction the Louisiana Purchase. There would be no need for an appeal to the people for an amendment either before or after the fact. Jefferson might simply declare that what he had done was not only justified by the benefits of the purchase but perfectly legal as well. "Upon an examination of the constitution," Nicholas wrote,

> I find the power as broad as it could well be made (3d par. 4 art.), except that new States cannot be formed out of the old ones without the consent of the State to be dismembered; and the exception is a proof to my mind that it was not intended to confine the congress in the admission of new States to what was then the territory of the U.S. Nor do I see anything in the constitution that limits the treaty-making power, except the general limitation of the power given to the government, and the evident object for which the government was instituted.

Jefferson at first seemed to disagree. "I had rather ask an enlargement of power from the nation, when it is found necessary," Jefferson stated, "than to assume it by a construction which would make our powers boundless." In the end, though, Jefferson relented: "If . . . our friends shall think differently, certainly I acquiesce with satisfaction; confiding, that the good sense of our country will correct the evil of construction when it shall produce ill effects" (26–28).

Jefferson's final stance was a compromise. He did not openly profess a trespass against the Constitution. Saint Thomas of Monticello might have done so and invited the people to consider impeachment as the appropriate sanction should they have felt punishment was called for. President Jefferson, by contrast, was content with virtual silence. He urged his friends to whom he had written regarding an amendment to hold in confidence the president's counsel, and the president avoided speaking publicly on the issue. In only one address, in fact, did President Jefferson discuss the purchase in a substantive way. On that occasion, moreover, he publicly asserted that which he privately doubted, the constitutionality of the purchase, and avoided any invitation to debate. When the treaty documents, Jefferson stated, "shall have received the constitutional sanction of the Senate, they will without delay be communicated to the Representatives also for the exercise of their functions as to those conditions which are within the powers vested by the Constitution in Congress." Elsewhere in this address, in acknowledging the increase in the public debt which the purchase would entail, Jefferson again implicitly proclaimed the constitutionality of the nation's augmentation. "Should the acquisition of Louisiana be constitutionally confirmed and carried into effect," Jefferson remarked, the public debt would be increased.[39]

Even Jefferson's critics did not make much of an issue of the constitutionality of his acts. A Federalist did comment in congressional debate, "It seems the powers that be concern themselves little about the Constitution. The *fact* that the treaty is carried into effect is enough for them."[40] But the Federalists were themselves broad constructionists and risked exposing their own programs to criticism (and themselves to ridicule) were they to charge the president with constitutional impropriety. Instead, most Federalists contented themselves with praising the deed while attempting to deny credit to the president and his party.[41]

For their part, Jefferson's supporters followed their president and declined to discuss any more than necessary the relationship of means to ends. Many tried, in fact, to strengthen the president's resolve to avoid acknowledging the magnitude of his break with constitutional principles. "The cession makes no alteration in the Constitution," Thomas Paine wrote from France; "it only extends the principles of it over a larger territory, and this certainly is within the morality of the Constitution."[42] Paine's implied distinction between the "morality" of the Constitution and what the Constitution actually says was beside the point. The president's act was highly popular; was of unmistakably great magnitude; and was consummated in full light of public scrutiny. The people knew what had been done, who had done it, and why. Their widespread acquiescence in Jefferson's constitutional sleight of hand was appropriately deferential.

The Louisiana Purchase followed, if prospectively, Locke's fundamental law of nature and government: self-preservation. The purchase was not for the sake of personal glory. It was not even necessarily in the interest of national expansion. Jefferson was content, that is, to envision Louisiana's eventual settlement by independent *sister republics.* The incorporation of Louisiana into the compact of states was not a necessary part of the greatness of what Jefferson had accomplished. Rather, the purchase, as he saw it, guaranteed long into the future the integrity of the United States as it existed at the time.[43] Abraham Lincoln's exercise of prerogative was similarly, if less rigidly, circumscribed.

ABRAHAM LINCOLN

"In this act, discarding all else," Lincoln said of the Confederates' attack on Fort Sumter, "they have forced upon the country the distinct issue, 'Immediate dissolution or blood.'" Lincoln chose blood. He did so, he said, because the issue embraced "more than the fate of these United States." The whole fate of republican government, he asserted, rested on a Union victory. Lincoln's historical claim was highly dubious. Consider freedom for slaves; slaves in North America would most likely have won their freedom sooner had the United States never existed! And is the history of republican government in Canada, Australia, or Great Britain itself any less inspiring than the history of public liberty in the United States? The differences are surely of degree, not kind. But, for reasons analyzed in Chapter One, Lincoln naturally read into the conflict millennial hopes and fears. "So viewing the issue," Lincoln continued, "no choice was left but to call out the war power of the Government and so resist force employed for its destruction by force for its preservation."[44]

The statement "no choice was left" was in this instance tantamount to that other great expression of the spirit of prerogative: "Who wills the end, wills the means." The end was the preservation of union. The means employed by Lincoln constitute the longest list of prerogative acts ever taken by an American executive. In an executive order of February 14, 1862, releasing political prisoners held in military custody, Lincoln himself provided a partial listing of his extraordinary measures. "In this emergency," Lincoln said, using the third-person voice, the president

> called into the field such military and naval forces as seemed necessary. He directed measures to prevent the use of the post-office for treasonable correspondence. He subjected passengers to and from foreign countries to new passport regulations, and he instituted a blockade, suspended the writ of habeas corpus in various places, and caused persons who were represented to him as being or about to engage in disloyal and treasonable practices to be arrested by special civil as well as military agencies and detained in military custody. (3304)

Before the war was over, Lincoln additionally promulgated a code of laws for the conduct of armies in the field, instituted conscription without congressional authorization, confiscated citizens' property, suppressed the press, and proclaimed freedom for slaves. His assumed powers stretched beyond any reasonable construal of the boundaries of executive power under the Constitution. Lincoln exercised not only powers that were arguably inherent in the executive article; he asserted control over functions that plainly belonged to other branches of government.[45]

Were such extraordinary means truly necessary? Lincoln answered this question in a parable tucked into his first annual message. "It has been said," Lincoln wrote to the Congress,

> that one bad general is better than two good ones, [that] an army is better directed by a single mind, though inferior, than by two superior ones at variance and cross-purposes with each other. And the same is true of all joint operations wherein those engaged can have none but a common end in view and can differ only as to the choice of means. In a storm at sea no one on board can wish the ship to sink, and yet not infrequently all go down together because too many will direct and no single mind can be allowed to control.[46]

The Congress, the cabinet, and all the other second-guessers may have chosen differently in each instance in which Lincoln felt compelled to act. But if they wished for the Union to be preserved, it was best that they trust Lincoln not to err too badly in deciding how to do it, lest they lose the opportunity for victory. If mistakes were made along the way, that was unavoidable. Someone had to act; who better than the only government authority in whom all the people of the nation had learned to see themselves potentially embodied?

Lincoln waffled on the legality of his acts, at some points seeming to concede that they were not "strictly legal,"[47] at others insisting that they were as legally pure as they were morally expedient. Lincoln's broadest claim, that the president possesses a constitutional "war power" wrought of the union of the commander-in-chief role and the executive's duty to execute the laws, has not persuaded critics of prerogative. As constitutional scholar Raoul Berger writes: "So far as the original meaning and intention are concerned, neither power taken alone conferred a 'war-making power,' and when nothing is added to nothing the sum remains nothing."[48] Lincoln's attempt to clothe with the propriety of law his decision to emancipate the slaves was equally hollow. In issuing the Emancipation Proclamation, the president undermined an institution that was explicitly protected by the Constitution and whose regulation was entrusted to the Congress. Lincoln also deprived slave owners of property without due process of law and thereby violated the Fifth Amendment to the Constitution. Furthermore, as Richard Pious has noted, "If Lincoln wished to argue that emancipation was a war measure, then under the rules of international law the property of enemy citizens on land was exempt from seizure without compensation."[49] Lincoln's defense, in a letter to a political associate, was that "measures, otherwise unconstitutional, might become lawful, by becoming indispensable to the preservation of the constitution, through the preservation of the nation."[50] This was Lincoln the lawyer speaking. An illegal act cannot *become* lawful at some later date. It may be pardonable and even praiseworthy; it cannot change its status under the law. Lincoln offered a similarly legalistic argument when he asserted that his oath of office, in which he swore to "preserve, protect, and defend the Constitution," required him to violate that document in order to uphold it.

Despite these attempts to define away the extraordinary nature of his acts, Lincoln's implied standard of popular judgment on all occasions was the same and was highly appropriate. The end plainly in sight for Lincoln during the war was to preserve the nation and its promise for the future as foretold in the country's civil religion. Because the people judged his character and intentions to be sound, they acquiesced in his actions and in fact returned the president to office.

This was prerogative government. That it was our form of government while the war lasted was in large measure the consequence of Lincoln's preference for blood over dissolution. Lincoln, once in office, might have followed Buchanan's pacific course or heeded the advice of Secretary of State Seward, who suggested a compromise with the South and a war against Mexico to rally the nation.[51] Though Lincoln was not above noting with satisfaction the public's approval of his extraordinary actions, he did not seek to justify himself on the grounds of a Jacksonian mandate from the people. The choice was his, and we should not be so blinded by Lincoln's place in our nation's history to recognize that he did in fact have a choice to make. This is easy to overlook for a number of reasons, not least of which is the simple fact that the North won the war and that several generations have passed since that time. We should also be thankful, however, that the man who did choose war was a man like Lincoln. That Lincoln's rulership did not involve even greater reliance upon prerogative is largely due, as James Randall has written, to Lincoln's "dislike of arbitrary rule, his reasonableness in practical judgment, and his disinclination toward military excess."[52] Like George Washington, Abraham Lincoln proved his tremendous worth as a ruler through his restraint. Both men could probably have established themselves at the head of a Napoleonic regime. Both preferred not to. Franklin Roosevelt was no Bonaparte either, but he came closer to the mark.

FRANKLIN ROOSEVELT

Franklin Roosevelt's most audacious exercise of prerogative occurred during the prelude to America's entry into World War II. By executive agreement, on September 2, 1940, Roosevelt gave to Great Britain fifty American destroyers. In "exchange," the United States agreed to operate for the British several Caribbean bases. This deal violated the Neutrality Act passed earlier that year, which prohibited the transfer of usable military equipment to other nations, as well as a 1917 law prohibiting the use of American warships by a belligerent power. The president's attorney general offered specious constructions of these statutes in defense of the president's acts but rested the president's defense most squarely on the alleged "plenary powers of the President as Commander-in-Chief of the Army and Navy and as head of state in its relations with foreign countries." The Congress was, in any event, not prepared to join battle with the president over his policies. Many senators were in fact pleased "that Roosevelt had let them off the hook."[53] Roosevelt continued to rely upon prerogative power throughout 1941, granting aid to the Allied powers and steering the nation toward war. The president went so far as to begin an undeclared naval war, ordering American battleships to protect convoys on the open seas by attempting to sink Axis submarines. In September, the president instituted a "shoot on sight" policy, and in October the navy was given orders to destroy Axis ships even if they were nowhere near British convoys (55). These actions and the principles that informed them had been prefigured in Roosevelt's first inaugural address, when he asked the people to support him in his "war" against the Great Depression.

Lead, follow, or get out of the way. This was Franklin Roosevelt's message to the Congress on assuming the presidency. "I am prepared," Roosevelt stated in his inaugural,

> to recommend the measures that a stricken Nation in the midst of a stricken world may require. These measures, or such other measures as the Congress may build out of its experience and wisdom, I shall seek, within my constitutional authority, to bring to speedy adoption. But in the event that the Congress shall fail to take one of these two courses, and in the event that the national emergency is still critical, I shall not evade the clear course of duty that will then confront me. I shall ask the Congress for the one remaining instrument to meet the crisis–broad Executive power to wage a war against the emergency, as great as the power that would be given to me if we were in fact invaded by a foreign foe.[54]

Eleanor Roosevelt, observing that this passage from her husband's speech received the most enthusiastic public response, called the whole ceremony "very, very solemn and a little terrifying."[55] Whether they were terrified or not, the president knew, as he stated elsewhere in this speech, that the people would support him; the people, Roosevelt proclaimed in the same address, wanted "action, and action now." And what sort of action did the president propose to take?

Roosevelt's domestic program has properly been termed a revolution. In the New Deal, the government went beyond a point of no return in the centralization of responsibility for the nation. The national government, through a complex array of new agencies, most of them created by executive fiat, thereby established for the first time "a [lasting] direct and coercive relationship between itself and individual citizens."[56] This was the meaning of such innovations in government as the Agricultural Adjustment Administration, the National Labor Relations Board, the Federal Trade Commission, and the Farm Security Administration. In his inaugural, Roosevelt elaborated on his confident assumption that the people would welcome this type of action even though it meant assuming new obligations as taxpayers, producers, laborers, employers, employees, and citizens. The key was the people's dawning awareness, which Progressives in American politics had long foretold, that the age of unmitigated individualism was at an end.

> If I read the temper of our people correctly, we now realize as we have never realized before our interdependence on each other; that we cannot merely take but we must give as well; that if we are to go forward, we must move as a trained and loyal army willing to sacrifice for the good of a common discipline, because without such discipline no progress is made, no leadership becomes effective. We are, I know, ready and willing to submit our lives and property to such discipline, because it makes possible a leadership which aims at a larger good. This I propose to offer, pledging that the larger purposes will bind upon us all as a sacred obligation with a unity of duty hitherto evoked only in time of armed strife.[57]

The people, Roosevelt intuited, wanted not only action but discipline.

Discipline of the self and its desires was the very foundation of the cooperative commonwealth envisioned by Roosevelt and his famous brain trusters. Rexford Tugwell, a member of this advisory group, published an aptly titled work in the same year that Roosevelt became president. In *The Industrial Discipline and the Govern-*

mental Arts, Tugwell wrote, "What is required in view of the nature of industry is a recognition of the desirability of large scale and of concentration. . . . Such a recognition would cause us to abandon attempts to prevent association and to enforce conflict."[58] The individualist pursuit of gain led to conflict, and conflict was wasteful and obsolete. Humankind was competing itself right into the ground, struggling to maintain an ethos of individualism which, with the closing of the frontier and the "maturation" of the nation's industry, had become destructive rather than ennobling. "The individual," Tugwell argued in 1932, "to get anywhere himself, must subordinate himself, must sink or swim with others. He must consent to function as part of a greater whole and to have his role defined for him by the exigencies of his group."[59] In a speech that Roosevelt delivered on September 23, 1932, on the campaign trail, the candidate expressed similar views. "Our task now," he told the audience at San Francisco's Commonwealth Club, "is not discovery or exploitation of natural resources, or necessarily producing more goods. It is the soberer, less dramatic business of administering resources and plants already in hand; of adjusting production to consumption; of distributing wealth and products equitably; of adapting existing economic organizations to the service of the people." Who would do these wondrous things; who would enlarge the scope of the people's positive freedom? The government administrator, who would sit astride an executive establishment that was not a countervailing but an overriding power. "The day of the manager has come," Roosevelt announced in this speech.[60]

In return for the discipline for which they longed, the people would grant their maximum manager their trust. Trust was crucial because the transformation toward more cooperative and less competitive ways of living was going to be difficult and intellectually, if not physically, painful. It was going to require the sacrifice of tired but trusted pieties about government's relationship to business and society. First, Roosevelt would have to rethink the rights of the people:

> Government is a relation of give and take, a contract, perforce, if we would follow the thinking out of which it grew. Under such a contract rulers were accorded power, and the people consented to that

> power on consideration that they be accorded certain rights. The task of statesmanship has always been the redefinition of these rights in terms of a changing and growing social order.[61]

Lincoln, of course, had acted in this manner when declaring emancipation for slaves in rebel territory. In explaining his action to the people, he stressed military necessity, as well as the fitness of his deed in light of what he famously proclaimed to be the nation's founding document, the Declaration of Independence. In judging his actions, Lincoln invited the people to consult this fundamental document of the polity. Roosevelt implied that the statesman was not to be bound by such concerns. "New conditions impose new requirements upon Government and those who conduct government" (ibid.).

Roosevelt never clarified by what standard the statesman should be guided in declaring new rights to the people. During the campaign, as historians have long noted, Roosevelt was vague and contradictory about his philosophy of government. In Robert Eden's interpretation of the philosophical underpinnings of the New Deal, Roosevelt's refusal to state a coherent philosophy was an expression of Roosevelt's view of statesmanship, which included the maxim that the president should be independent from the constraints of public philosophy and even from traditional understandings of public morality.[62]

In his Commonwealth Club address, Roosevelt established a parallel between the state-building efforts of the early European monarchs and the task that awaited the next president.

> The growth of the national Governments of Europe was a struggle for the development of a centralized force in the Nation, strong enough to impose peace upon ruling barons. In many instances the victory of the central Government, the creation of a strong central Government, was a haven of refuge to the individual. The people preferred the master far away to the exploitation and cruelty of the smaller master nearer at hand.
>
> But the creators of national Government were perforce ruthless men.[63]

The ruthlessness of centralizing monarchs was necessary in its day. The ruthlessness of industrializing trusts and "robber barons," Roosevelt continued, had been necessary in the period that closed with the Great Depression. And to subdue the now obsolete titans of industry and finance would *perforce* require the executive to wield new powers. American life was now and forever "corporate," and executive power would have to be brought to bear upon the government, upon business, upon individuals, to realign American life to this fact.

Roosevelt's assertion of prerogative power, like Lincoln's, was open ended. Unlike Lincoln and Jefferson, however, Roosevelt did not ask that the people consult the founding principles of the nation in determining whether to place their trust in him. The difference was in both circumstances and personal inclination. Roosevelt's crisis was the most confusing and intangible; his response was (perforce?) the most innovative. Prerogative is typically used to *save* something of obvious value: a person's life, a nation's security, or territorial or spiritual integrity. Roosevelt's New Deal was rather an act of creative destruction: destroying the foundations of laissez-faire capitalism and the old individualism in law and public morality, calling forth a new order whose dimensions he was content to measure, not dictate.

The crucial Rooseveltian innovation was, then, the emphasis he placed on the people's trust in themselves rather than in their nation as the wellspring of popular trust in the president. (Conservatives soon learned to speak in this vein: "In your heart, you know he's right.") Consult your own feelings, Roosevelt implored the people. If you do so, you will surely decide to put your faith in me. Why? Because I will give to you those things that are so basic and fundamental to humanity that anyone who has already lost them, or who can imagine the anguish of such a loss, will thrill to the idea that they might be secured for every deserving person, once and for all. What things? Freedom from want, from hunger, from privation, from fear itself. This message was reassuring precisely because it played upon fears that had been tremendously enhanced during the Great Depression and because it wrapped new positive freedoms or responsibilities in the more comfortable idiom of negative freedoms: freedom *from* constraints, rather than freedom *for* collective action. But how far should the executive be allowed to go? How exclusively should the redefinition of rights be entrusted to the president?

Roosevelt recognized that his programs had raised such questions. In a private meeting with his National Emergency Council, the seat of prerogative government early in his administration, the president remarked:

> There are individuals who want $500 to start raising chickens, and from there up to the corporation that wants to borrow money to meet its payroll; from there up to the railroad that has to refund its bonds coming due; from there up to the municipality that says the wicked banks won't let us have any money; and from there down to the individual who says he is entitled to work. . . . There is a general feeling that it is up to the government to take care of everybody, financially and otherwise. . . . One brass band asked to be financed on a trip around the country.[64]

What could be done? Roosevelt's suggestion was instructive of the dilemma that he had created. The people were making demands that the president found ridiculous precisely because he had made such open-ended promises to care for them. The trust they had given him was in return for discipline, but discipline for what purpose, and for whom? Why *not* try to find discipline in a brass band? What needed to be done, the president said, was simple: "Somebody ought to give an awfully mean talk–a thoroughly mean, hard-boiled talk–about the things they cannot expect. Otherwise, it will cause us more trouble down here." Who should give the talk? Somebody other than the president, of course. "Will you try to arrange to have somebody do that?" Roosevelt asked his Emergency Council (77).

CONCLUSION

The "great" presidents, it is sometimes said, proved themselves by meeting crises. But this understates the role each of them played in creating the context in which he would later be judged. They not only "met" crises; they helped to create them. That this was so in the case of Andrew Jackson was made clear in Chapters One and Four. And the historian John Morton Blum has demonstrated how Woodrow Wilson, through "the ratchet of his rhetoric," contributed to the onset of hostilities between the United States and Germany.[65] Wilson's interpretation of the war's meaning, moreover, was highly personal, and he pursued peace as well as war at considerable cost to the nation and himself. In electing great men to the presidency, the people get more than they perhaps asked for. This was definitely the case with the three "greats" discussed in this chapter. That most of us judge the country to have been well served by Jefferson's, Lincoln's, and Roosevelt's use of discretionary authority should not obscure the potential for abuse in this arrangement.

The principal restraint on the assertion of prerogative turns out to be moral character. Presidents Jefferson, Lincoln, and Roosevelt, it is commonly agreed, were exceptional men. They were keenly aware of their responsibilities to the nation, and they, at the very least, meant well when they overstepped the bounds of the Constitution. Their example can be contrasted with that of Nixon, discussed in Chapter Three. The great majority of the American people, in the end, judged Nixon to be a pretender to the throne. He lacked the requisite personal qualities to exercise vast powers: the disinterestedness and the other-directedness of the presidents focused upon immediately above. And the example of Harry Truman, discussed early in this chapter, is similarly instructive. The public deemed him, too, unfit for the mantle worn by the "greats." These counterexamples suggest that the people do set bounds about executive discretion. Prerogative is not to be used for the personal glory or partisan advantage of the president. Exactly how it may be used, however, is for the most part up to presidents to decide.

6

WANTED: HEROES IN THE WHITE HOUSE

THE DELEGATES TO THE CONSTITUTIONAL CONVENTION intended the president to be a leader, but they could not have meant for him to exercise leadership. The word *leadership*, which means the ability to lead, was not in use when the *Federalist* papers were written. Its first usage, according to the *Oxford English Dictionary*, dates from 1821. But what is a leader, if not one who possesses or practices leadership? The historian Edmund Morgan explains this paradox in his analysis of the delegates' design of government. "The size of the new nation," they believed, would make it difficult for the "politicians of the states to assemble a majority faction. Control of government would then return to the public spirited members of the better sort who alone would have the national renown to win elections in a continental contest, without regard to the talents that lesser men might devote to winning votes."[1] In eighteenth-century America, before the development of mass-based parties, leaders led by consequence of their social standing. Truly great leaders were men of superior social rank who were fortunate enough to secure an opportunity to display their virtue and thus secure for posterity their just portion of fame.

This vision of leaders without leadership can be found in *Federalist* paper 71, in which Hamilton argues for the independence of the executive. From today's vantage point, Hamilton's argument is as strange in its content as in its syntax. To be appreciated, it must be quoted at length:

> It is a just observation that the people commonly *intend* the PUBLIC GOOD. This often applies to their very errors. But their good sense would despise the adulator who should pretend that they always *reason right* about the *means* of promoting it. They know from experience that they sometimes err; and the wonder is that they so seldom err as they do, beset as they continually are by the wiles of parasites and sycophants, by the snares of the ambitious, the avaricious, the desperate, by the artifices of men who possess their confidence more than they deserve it. When occasions present themselves in which the interests of the people are at variance with their inclinations, it is the duty of the persons whom they have appointed to be the guardians of those interests to withstand the temporary delusion in order to give them time and opportunity for more cool and sedate reflection. Instances may be cited in which a conduct of this kind has saved the people from very fatal consequences of their own mistakes, and has procured lasting monuments of their gratitude to the men who had courage and magnanimity enough to serve them at the peril of their displeasure.[2]

The good ruler, Hamilton implies, acts so as to deserve the people's esteem. If he fails to attain it, he must understand that the people sometimes err, and hope that future generations will be more grateful to him than were his contemporaries.

Our earliest presidents acted as if instructed by Hamilton's implied lesson on presidential craft. Our first and our third presidents were honored as great men while they held office but were revered all the more after their deaths. Our second president has still not won an equal measure of his nation's gratitude but demonstrated nevertheless an unbending concern for posterity as president.[3] These men, indeed all our presidents up to Andrew Jackson, were charter members of the better sort. (Even Jackson, a member of the Scots-Irish ascendancy, was not as socially distant from his predecessors as his popular image might indicate.)[4] As presidents, highborn men were expected neither to beg nor to buy the favors of the people. For their part, citizens in the early republic were deferential, seldom even voting in presidential elections. (What proportion of voters, one wonders, did not vote because they were uncomfortable at the thought of passing judgment upon a social superior?)

The rise of democracy and the civil-religious sanctioning of partisan conflict effaced the early American conjunction of social status and rulership. Even after the 1830s, however, nineteenth-century presidents continued to be influenced by the ideas of the founding generation. It was widely believed, for instance, that it was beneath the dignity of a presidential candidate to seek the office that he may in fact have been lusting for all his life. William McKinley's front-porch campaign of 1896, in which 750,000 people traveled to Canton, Ohio, to pay their respects to the candidate, offered spectacular proof of the resilience of this taboo in the face of ever-advancing transportation and communications technology. (Think how much more efficient it would have been for the candidate to have visited the voters!)[5]

Despite the continued observance of the ban on electioneering, presidents, from the 1830s on, had to practice leadership if they were to lead. At the least, this meant that each president had to be a fit symbol of partisan unity and purpose. At the most, presidents such as Jackson and Lincoln might speak to the people indirectly, through their messages to Congress, and thereby mobilize the nation in pursuit of an arduous task, such as war. It was only after the examples of Wilson and the two Roosevelts, however, that leadership came to be regarded as an essential ingredient to a successful presidency. How particular modern presidents handled their leadership task, and how presidents more generally should do their job, are thus the subjects of what is by now a vast scholarly literature.

FOUR PERSPECTIVES ON PRESIDENTIAL LEADERSHIP

If Franklin Roosevelt is the patron saint of presidential leadership studies, the part of devil has often been assigned to Dwight Eisenhower. The apparent lack of presidential leadership in the 1950s, for example, struck Dartmouth political scientist Robert Carr as evidence of a crisis in the public's spirit. "Can we yet come through this crisis of nerve with the power and the glory of the Presidency unabated?" he asked. "Clearly this is a moment when we desperately need from our best scholars and wisest commentators a careful and dispassionate re-examination of the Presidency and its true tradition as a great and powerful office."[6] Carr answered his question with a tentative yes, thanks to noted presidency scholars Edward Corwin, Louis Koenig, and Clinton Rossiter, whose works Carr reviewed for the *New York Times*. These men's books, Carr wrote, described "the almost miraculous emergence of a monolithic, powerful Presidency." Four years later, *New York Times* editorialist Tom Wicker phrased his compliments to Richard Neustadt, author of the classic *Presidential Power: The Politics of Leadership*, with similar contempt for the general-turned-president. Declining even to accord the man his rightful title, Wicker wrote that General Eisenhower had helped to prove that the White House was "no place for a political amateur." Neustadt's book left "no such illusion."[7]

Ordinary Americans liked Ike just fine. But to liberal intellectuals, Eisenhower seemed a throwback to the ancients. He, like the presidents of the founding generation and their unworthy epigones, subscribed to the theory that presidents should preside over a government rather than lead a people. President Eisenhower's second-term response to the intellectuals' call for leadership was to empanel a national commission. The commission, in the president's words, was to "set up a series of goals" for Americans.[8] In light of the revisionist scholarship of Fred Greenstein, we can appreciate the political savvy of this transfer of authority, but Eisenhower's seeming refusal to take personal responsibility for the nation's well-being did not sit well with contemporary commentators.[9] The critique of Eisenhower's leadership, expressed most influentially in Neustadt's volume, in fact remains a cornerstone of one of the leading schools of thought on presidential leadership. But before saying more about the Neustadtian school, I want to locate it within the context of contemporary political science thinking on presidential leadership more generally.

Of the half-dozen or so major perspectives on presidential craft, I focus on four. These four can be distinguished one from the other by the emphasis their authors place on the resources for and objectives of the president's task as leader. With regard to resources, some observers believe that a president must derive his authority principally from personal qualities, such as his skill at bargaining. To others, the presidency is inescapably a constitutional office, whose occupant, to be successful, must seek his power in the attributes of his office as it was established in 1787. With regard to the objectives of presidential leadership, scholars tend to emphasize either the managerial or moral ends that presidents pursue. Table 1 displays the four schools of thought which emerge from these contrasting emphases, with representative works on the office positioned in their appropriate places. Moving clockwise from the upper left cell in this table, the four positions can be characterized as personal managerialism, personal moralism, constitutional moralism, and constitutional managerialism.[10] The seven representative books that appear in the table were authored by five political scientists and a jurist.

THE PRESIDENT AS A PERSONAL-MANAGERIAL LEADER

Richard Neustadt's *Presidential Power* was first published in 1960 and last updated thirty years later. The book expresses its author's self-professed desire to "snuggle up" to politics in his work as a teacher and writer, "to look at power close up, to see how it can be used."[11] From the moment a new president takes the oath of office, Neustadt wrote in the preface to the original edition of his classic work, "the man confronts a personal problem: how to make [the presidency's] powers work for *him*." This "search for personal influence," Neustadt asserted, "is at the center of the job of being President." Consequently, "to analyze the problem of obtaining personal power one must try to view the Presidency from over the President's shoulder, looking out and down with the perspective of his place."[12] From this start, Neustadt went on to develop his well-known argument that presidential power is the power to persuade. Because, furthermore, the American government is one of "separated institutions sharing powers," the power to persuade is the power to bargain. To leave his personal mark on the politics and policies of his time, a president must be a consummate deal

Table 1: Some Leading Interpretations of Presidential Leadership

RESOURCES	OBJECTIVES	
	Managerial	**Moral**
Personal	*Presidential Power* by R. Neustadt	*Leadership* *The Power to Lead* by J. Burns
Constitutional	*The Personal President* by T. Lowi	*The Rhetorical Presidency* by J. Tulis
	The American Presidency by R. Pious	*Energy in the Executive* by T. Eastland

maker. But he must not get so immersed in any one deal that he unwittingly sacrifices his future power to the exigencies of the moment. In the bargains he strikes, that is, one concern must be paramount: to calculate the power stakes of the decisions that he makes. At each step in the development of this argument, Neustadt illustrates his points with examples of presidential decision making, often pitting the politically astute Franklin Roosevelt and the uneven Harry Truman against the amateurish Dwight Eisenhower.

Neustadt's work has been criticized for its allegedly Machiavellian disregard for morality. In Thomas Cronin's words, "The imperative [in Neustadt's book] for assertive, ambitious leadership overshadows any hint that a president's objectives might be deficient."[13] Neustadt replies to his critics in the preface to the 1990 edition of his book. "I persist," he writes, "in the belief . . . that pursuit of presidential power . . . is good for the country," as well as for the president. Presidential leadership helps "to energize" the government in pursuit of policies "with staying power." And if the policies are not those Neustadt favors, "so be it."[14] Neustadt's quasi-Hamiltonian pronouncement that energy in administration is the paramount objective of the presidency may seem cavalier, but it accurately reflects the Democratic liberal worldview of the 1950s and beyond. A central tenet of that belief system is that the sheer "velocity of history," to quote from Arthur Schlesinger Jr., will make bitter controversies over principles obsolete. The highest morality is thus the amorality of the expert administrator.[15] To more intense liberals, as well as conservatives, the assumption that administrative energy is the end of leadership is highly suspect. Thus James McGregor Burns, though he shares Neustadt's concern for the personal basis of power, claims the moral high ground in his treatment of presidential leadership.

THE PRESIDENT AS A PERSONAL-MORAL LEADER

"Endless presidential bargaining, persuading, power-hoarding, managing, manipulating–is this executive *leadership*?" Burns asks in reviewing Neustadt's argument.[16] Burns' answer is: not for the kind of president this nation needs. The best kind of leadership, according to Burns, is "transforming": It aims at "sustained and planned social transformation" (396); it "raises the level of human conduct and ethical aspiration of both leader and led" (20). Transforming leadership in the presidency is desperately needed, Burns wrote in 1984, to permit the as-yet-unknown leader and his or her followers to "transcend" the concerns of the moment and to "reconstruct the political system" so that it responds positively to "fundamental human needs and American values."[17]

Burns' understanding of fundamental human needs is decidedly partisan. "Why place the burden of such [transforming] change on the Democrats?" he asks. Because the Republicans, under Reagan, became an effective but "narrow, negative, and reactionary" party. Anyway, "it is not the job of conservatives to be innovators, institution changers, reformers. That is the job of liberals, leftists, and radicals" (242). A leftist president, at the head of a class-conscious Democratic party, is the only force, Burns believes, which can save the nation. The leadership of men like Thomas Jefferson and Franklin Roosevelt partook of this quality. Not every president need be of their caliber. Transforming leadership, Burns recognizes, is like a fire in a wooden stockade–it can kill even while it liberates. But, Burns is certain, it is what this nation must have now.

Ironically, because Burns' conception of America's moral potentialities is as vague as, if more radical than, Neustadt's, Burns' complex argument builds to an anticlimax. Presidents must be brave and high-minded, Burns teaches us, but we are left wondering how to tell a high-minded from a low-minded call to "Follow Me!" The same can be said of James David Barber's *Presidential Character.*[18] Barber analyzes presidents in terms of how active they are and how they feel about their work. Those who are very energetic and who enjoy being president are classified as "active-positives." Such presidents have high self-esteem and are flexible and adaptive in matching means to ends. The active-negative president, by contrast, works hard but does not derive personal satisfaction from his efforts. Woodrow Wilson, Lyndon Johnson, and Richard Nixon were presidents shaped in this mold. They meant well, but they were rigid in their thinking. As a consequence, they could not cope when things did not go their way. Passive presidents, like Dwight Eisenhower and Ronald Reagan, are also not suited to be president. This, Barber believes, is so obvious that had the voters been wise to Reagan's passive-positive character, "they might have voted him down" (224). To do the job right today simply requires more energy than a passive man (or woman) can bring to the task. The best presidents, then, are those like Jefferson, Franklin Roosevelt, and John Kennedy: whirlwinds of energy with a passion for politics.

What is moral about all this energy and passion? The active-positive president, Barber answers, is a moral adventurer. He does not try to master the future "by some mechanical application of 'principles,' but by imaginative experimentation." The active-positive president stimulates and invigorates the people and energizes "their own positive imaginations." For his most dedicated followers, he is a charismatic icon; for nearly everyone "he supplies a sense that he is at the center of fascinating events and that the center is moving" (267–68). Barber, like Burns, praises presidents who stimulate the public to a new, but undefined, consciousness of their needs. If the moral of Burns' work is that presidents should be high-minded, the moral of Barber's is that they must be so energetically and with unfeigned pleasure.

THE PRESIDENT AS A CONSTITUTIONAL-MORAL LEADER

The constitutional, as opposed to the personal, moralists concur with Burns and Barber that the good president pursues good goals. Terry Eastland, director of public affairs at the Justice Department under President Reagan, believes that the good president, by exercising strictly constitutional powers as opposed to the personal powers emphasized by Neustadt, Burns, and Barber, "defends against attacks upon any aspect of his power. He can, that is, and he should. Imposed by [constitutional] design upon individual Presidents is a substantive public policy: vigilant defense of the office itself. The Constitution equips and asks Presidents to be strong, for their own sake but also that of good government."[19] The Constitution, Eastland reminds us, grants the president specific powers. By making full use of such powers as the veto, the right to "litigate the agenda" (i.e., take Congress to court in defense of alleged usurpations of executive power), the right to appoint the members of the federal courts, and the alleged right to take the nation to war, the president may beat the opposition. And he may do so without either stooping to the level of Neustadt's bargainer-in-chief or aspiring to the false heights of Burns' transformer-in-chief. From Eastland's perspective, when George Bush maneuvered the U.S. Congress into a position in which its assent to war was the only politically viable choice, he was acting as a constitutional executive should. He did not persuade; he acted. In acting, he gave energy to the government, and Eastland, ironically like Neustadt, is certain that "the best, most comprehensive way to talk about the Presidency is . . . in terms of energy" (ibid.). By linking energy to a vigorous assertion of constitutional powers, and by putting adherence to the Constitution at the center of "good government," Eastland seeks to ennoble the pursuit of presidential leadership.

Eastland draws heavily on the scholarship of Jeffrey Tulis, author of *The Rhetorical Presidency*.[20] Tulis's work is a major critique of twentieth-century presidents' absorption with rhetoric as the preeminent instrument of leadership. When presidents, as they now routinely do, address the people over the heads of Congress, they short-circuit the deliberative process. This, Tulis suggests, is demagoguery. The result of presidential demagoguery is congressional haste and executive-congressional chicanery. Bills are passed more for their momentary political impact than for posterity. Bad law and trickery, furthermore, contribute to a lack of trust between the people and their presidents, which presidents try to "fix" by yet more rhetoric. This circle of failure is all a consequence, Tulis argues, of the leadership style that presidents are now in the habit of using. When they get rhetorical, presidents wind up making promises they cannot possibly keep: a transcendence of power politics in the international arena, unconditional victory in a war against poverty, or a magical gain in tax revenues brought about by a reduction in tax rates.

Presidents can escape this desultory cycle, Tulis suggests, by harking back to the example of Theodore Roosevelt. Roosevelt loved to talk, Tulis acknowledges, but he was careful how he did so while he was president. His administration represents for Tulis a midway point between the old reliance on written messages from the president to Congress which were reprinted for the people and the new approach whereby presidents sic the people on a stigmatized Congress. Roosevelt, it seems, respected the Constitution's implied designation of Congress as the deliberative arm of government. Even when he appealed directly to the people for support, he timed his appeals so as not to usurp Congress's role in forging legislation. Presidents can, and sometimes even do, still act in this way. Ronald Reagan, Tulis and Eastland agree, was an exemplar of the right kind of presidential leadership in his campaign for tax reform. The president elevated the discussion of the tax code, they argue, by relating the proposed changes of the Tax Reform Act of 1986 to such issues as fairness and "law abidingness." The president, furthermore, refrained from bullying Congress, instead urging its members to decide the details of legislation for themselves. The battle for tax reform thus became a "vessel for regime-level debate" and a concrete "political reform."[21] Unfortunately for us, such high-minded restraint in the pursuit of presidential objectives is rare these days.

How might we change our political system to make the Theodore

Roosevelt approach more consistently appealing? Ironically, even if Tulis knew, he might not tell us. Tulis seems fearful, in fact, that if we strip from the contemporary presidency its rhetorical excesses, we might also thereby remove its leverage over the government in times of true emergency. When faced with a crisis, Tulis contends, a president must assert himself as the spokesperson of the nation. "The point cannot be stressed enough," he writes, "that the executive energy needed to contend with crisis is a genuine need for which the original Constitution may have inadequately provided."[22] Caught between the weakness of the old presidency and the demagoguery of the new, Tulis passes over in silence the critical question, How do we distinguish between true and false emergencies?

THE PRESIDENT AS A CONSTITUTIONAL-MANAGERIAL LEADER

Richard Pious and Theodore Lowi agree that presidential leadership should be constitutional leadership. Pious, in *The American Presidency*, argues that presidents must rely on their constitutional powers to lead because their personal resources for mobilizing the government—no matter how appealing their personalities—are few and contingent.[23] Especially today, with weak parties, mass abstention from voting, and a largely uncontrollable bureaucracy, "the fundamental and irreducible core of presidential power rests not on influence, persuasion, public opinion, elections, or party, but rather on the successful assertion of constitutional authority to resolve crises and significant domestic issues" (17). Only if he husbands his constitutional authority, including his prerogative power, can a president influence events.

As to the purpose that a president's constitutional leadership might advance, Pious is agnostic. Unlike Eastland, Pious is not certain that a constitutionally assertive president necessarily advances the cause of "good government." It depends in large part on the character of the other elected branch. "But as yet Congress has not demonstrated that it is prepared to assume a major role in a collaborative system" (421). Its preference is for reaction and acquiescence, punctuated by bursts of investigatory and obstructionist zeal. As a consequence of the political environment he finds himself in, the modern president who attempts a popular, partisan, bureaucratic, or collaborative strategy will likely do so in vain. When such strategies fail, presidents turn to unilateral assertions of constitutional authority. "Prerogatives are still seen by the White House as the antidote to paralysis" (422). The forecast, then, is for more of the same: more presidential-congressional conflict, and more assertions of a presidential right to govern alone. This, Pious believes, is not good government. The most we can hope for is a not-too-bad management of affairs in a state of perpetual government-induced crisis.

Theodore Lowi is even less optimistic. Lowi styles himself a proponent of "radical constitutionalism." The "litmus test" of this doctrine, he writes, is "putting concern for forms as equal to or above concern for power."[24] The form of the Constitution, Lowi believes, checks and balances congressional and presidential powers and does not sanction the presidency-centered government that he argues was a legacy of the Franklin Roosevelt administration. Lowi therefore critiques the works of Neustadt and Tulis as reflections, respectively, of liberal and neoconservative hero worship. Both works and the schools they represent, according to Lowi, seek to justify the modern president's usurpation of Congress's constitutional roles. To liberals and (ever since Reagan, at least) to many conservatives as well, Congress is the source of unnecessary deadlock (238).

Because "the presidency has gotten too big for the Constitution," presidents are trapped in futile attempts to live up to heroic conceptions of their office. The most that a reform-minded president might do on his own is to respect the Constitution and manage the government. As a first step, Lowi suggests that presidents veto bills that delegate legislative powers to the executive branch.[25]

HAVE THESE IDEAS HAD CONSEQUENCES?

At the beginning of this chapter, I noted the congruence between Hamilton's ideas and the behavior of our earliest chief executives.

Congruence, of course, does not say anything about causation, and I do not claim that Hamilton was the teacher and the presidents his pupils. Hamilton in any event did not make his remarks on the presidency in the context of writing a text for rulers but rather in the course of an argument addressed to those who would be ruled. Some of the literature reviewed above, by contrast, falls into the genre of didactic essays intended for the instruction of executives. Neustadt's and Eastland's books are explicitly designed to teach presidents and those who work for them (as both authors did) how to get the most out of presidential power. Burns', Tulis's and Lowi's books also contain instructions for presidents. Pious refrains from presuming to address presidents themselves but does articulate a vision of leadership which he implies would be appropriate for presidents to adopt. Barber, finally, addresses citizens, but lessons for presidents are easily deduced from his work.

For the most part, however, our princes have sought their reflections in other mirrors. The greatest exception is *Presidential Power*. Part of the fame of this book rests on the fact that its author has himself been close to the seat of power. After a stint in the Truman White House, Neustadt went on to advise Democratic presidents from Kennedy through Carter. Al Gore wrote his senior thesis under Professor Neustadt's guidance at Harvard University and has stayed in touch with his one-time academic adviser.[26]

Neustadt's most influential advice appears to have been given to John Kennedy, whom he urged to follow the lead of Franklin Roosevelt in organizing his White House staff. "Once you are 'Mr. President,'" Neustadt advised the president-elect, "nobody else can fully gauge your own, personal interests. In the last analysis, that is the 'staff job' for *you*."[27] Kennedy's style in office was certainly Rooseveltian: He kept his door open to an array of visitors and did not hesitate to reach into the bureaucracy to get information that his senior aides and cabinet members might–for their own reasons–not wish to bring to his attention. Most of all, he did everything with a great show of energy. But these attempts, if that is what they were, to follow Neustadt's advice bore bitter fruit in the Bay of Pigs and in the president's oft-lamented failures as a legislative leader.

Neustadt can no more be blamed for Kennedy's shortcomings,

however, than for those of Nixon's aides, who were admonished by Nixon's chief of staff, Bob Haldeman, to read *Presidential Power.* Neustadt's absolution is merited on two accounts. First there is Neustadt's dictum to recall: "*Yet nobody and nothing helps a President to see, save as he helps himself.*"[28] Not even the president's closest advisers share the president's singular perspective on events. If the president, for whatever reasons of personality or mere misfortune, miscalculates his power stakes and chooses badly what to pursue and when, that is his own fault. Secondly, there is Neustadt's own *mea culpa*: He did not imagine, he wrote in 1990, that such uneducated, inexperienced, and grasping men as occupied the Nixon White House would ever take him as their mentor (xvi–xvii). Put differently, Neustadt expected that future presidents would be either a little bit liberal, like Kennedy, or a little bit conservative, like Eisenhower. As such, they could be expected to understand that the benefits of maximizing presidential power in violent disregard of the civil rights and constitutional prerogatives of other persons in and out of government would never outweigh the costs. He anticipated, that is, neither Nixon's sense of persecution nor the Reaganites' revolutionary zeal.

Looking beyond Neustadt's influence, it seems that presidents since Kennedy have exhibited contrasting leadership styles but with little regard for the theories of political scientists. Nixon concentrated power within an ever-smaller staff and tried to outdo even his predecessor in his manic devotion to the work ethic. Carter's approach was contradictory. He dourly set himself to guarding the national interest but also sought to rely upon his appeal with the people. He attempted, that is, to be both a trustee and a populist, which proved as difficult in practice as it was implausible in theory.[29] President Carter did nonetheless claim during the 1976 election to have been influenced by several scholarly works, including James David Barber's *Presidential Character.* Barber himself, however, discounted the president-elect's assertion. Barber's typology has provided him with a platform from which to offer presidential endorsements every four years, and one suspects Carter of lobbying for support when he proclaimed himself an "active-positive." President Carter's grimness in office, in any event, showed that events can overwhelm dispositions (if

Carter and Barber, who concurred with the president-elect's self-assessment, if not his own influence on Carter's personality, were correct).[30] As for Ronald Reagan, it seems fair to say that the president taught political scientists more about leadership in the Oval Office than he learned from them.[31]

I wish not to deny the value of the literature reviewed above but to demonstrate its limited direct influence on its subject. Presidents have not learned how to lead by reading books on the topic. They are, however, subject to popular expectations about leadership which are themselves nourished by the political science literature. Ideas often influence their subjects indirectly, and that is the case here.

In terms of indirect influence, the personalist approaches represented by Neustadt, Burns, and Barber are most in accord with prevailing popular sentiments about the presidency. Two sentiments stand out. The first is the belief that direct appeals to the people should be at the core of a president's political strategy once in office. The second is that the president (each and every president) should aspire, in the peculiar language of Bill Clinton, to be a "change agent" in the tradition of Franklin Roosevelt. The most striking example of this is the rush to judgment which occurs just over three months into each new administration, in memory of Franklin Roosevelt's famed Hundred Days of legislative and executive action.[32]

Few presidents have been willing even to try to dampen expectations of a perpetually new-and-improved presidency. George Bush was, for a time, an exception. At his inauguration, he expressed his hope that his presidency would contribute but "a small and stately story" to the book of history. Bush's modest ambitions were suited to a man who won the presidency in an election dominated by valence issues and capped by a near-record low in electoral turnout for presidential contests. But Bush's sense of history, and his mature understanding that not every president can or should lead a revolution in policy, were not attuned to popular images of the office.[33]

The constitutionalist schools, by contrast, are far removed from popular visions of presidential leadership. Their potential influence is mitigated by their acknowledged distance from prevailing ideas and practices. Lowi, for instance, although he ends his volume on the presidency with prescriptions for institutional reforms that might "build down" presidential power to what he considers constitutional dimensions, writes that "real reform in American presidential government will not come until there is real change in the point of view of powerful people."[34] And a change in point of view, especially when that change goes against incentives and pressures found within the structures of everyday politics, is not an easy thing to bring about. In any event, what would happen politically to a president who attempted to reduce the people's expectations of his leadership? When President Carter, in July 1979, told the American people that they should look inward, instead of to their president, for the solution to what he perceived to be the country's crisis of spirit, his address was ridiculed as the "malaise" speech. Carter's talk, like John Quincy Adams' unfortunate first annual message to Congress, became a benchmark of political incompetence.

SO WHAT'S WRONG WITH HEROIC LEADERSHIP?

The popular expectation of heroic presidential leadership has been buoyed by political scientists who emphasize the personal and especially the moral aspects of their subject. Popular expectations have similarly been built up by our inability to discriminate among presidents and by the institutionalization within the White House of a permanent campaign apparatus of pollsters, media advisers, and speechwriters. The problem with expecting heroic leadership is not just that we invite disappointment. To get a clearer idea of the deficiency of the heroic model, imagine that we got what we seem to be asking for: each president a hero, each deserving of immortal fame. If we think back to the preceding chapter, we begin to see the problem. Our great presidents were great in the exercise of prerogative. They were crisis leaders, and in meeting crises, they were little checked in finding necessity where they chose to see it.[35] As a second step, we should pause to consider what, if anything, the nongreat presidents have contributed to the nation. Take, for a notable example, Dwight Eisenhower.

From the heroic leadership perspective, presidents such as Eisenhower occupy wasted time in the lineage of chief executives. The partisan argument against Eisenhower is clear enough. But was his leadership defective from a nonpartisan perspective? Eisenhower was quite successful in pursuing his major objective as president: a period of peace and a consequent reduction in military spending, troop levels, and government controls over the economy. Without Eisenhower's obstruction of his military advisers, manpower levels and controls might well have escalated much higher than they did during the Cold War. The United States might, in fact, have become a "garrison state," spending itself into economic exhaustion as did its superpower rival.[36] In addition, President Eisenhower, we now know, used a "hidden hand" approach to avoid the commitment of Americans to combat in Vietnam. Eisenhower was urged by his military advisers and by his party's leadership to come to the aid of the French at Dien Bien Phu in 1954. By making it appear as if his hands were tied by congressional caution and British reluctance to join with the United States, Eisenhower avoided a premature commitment to the defense of Vietnam.[37] At some times, there surely is a need for active leadership in the White House. But at other times, an obstructionist, even antileadership approach has its merits. If every president for the next several administrations actually were a heroic leader–persuading opponents and charming admirers, energizing the government to new heights of activism–the American people might remember what they (or perhaps their parents) liked about Eisenhower in the fifties.

To extend the thought experiment one step further, imagine that those twentieth-century presidents who most visibly yearned to be recalled for their heroic leadership had followed one another in office, with no interruptions from the less than heroic, and had been successful in the pursuit of their objectives. Teddy Roosevelt would have been followed by Woodrow Wilson, Franklin Roosevelt, Lyndon Johnson, finishing perhaps with Ronald Reagan. The display of personalities would have been dazzling. The government would have been buzzing with energy. And our government's policies, at home and abroad, would have been unstable, untested, and untrustworthy. With every change of administration, we would have "charted a new course" and experienced "real change." It is hard to see how the benefits of energy would have outweighed the costs of policy frenzy and instability.

Some recent books on the presidency are sensitive to the importance of history and timing. Arthur Schlesinger Jr., following the lead of his father, has put forth an argument based on mass psychology, to the effect that the American public can accommodate the stress of heroic leadership only so often. The people take breaks from doing good by electing to high office men as passive, inward-looking, and selfish as the people are at such moments. Schlesinger's view of history is linear. The movement of time is marked with a jagged line, sometimes progressing, sometimes stalling, but always moving in the same direction. From this perspective, a string of great presidents, if our psyche could handle it, would be a great thing, for it would permit us to reach the future sooner. The future, an elaboration upon the good qualities of the present, is hurried along by great presidents. If the limitations of this view of history were not apparent from the vast differences between the domestic policies of such men as Theodore Roosevelt and Woodrow Wilson, Harry Truman and John Kennedy, they are surely apparent now that Ronald Reagan has forced himself onto the list of presidents with great ambitions and considerable success. There is no single thread that connects and makes sense of all the ambitious presidencies.[38]

Political scientists Erwin Hargrove, Michael Nelson, and Stephen Skowronek have put forth more sophisticated arguments that attempt to specify the institutional as well as psychological conditions under which heroic presidential leadership becomes possible.[39] From the perspective of this historical school, presidents must understand the flow of history and be sensitive to their place in it. This is an important lesson. If it is widely disseminated, popular expectations of heroic leadership might usefully be diminished. At the moment, however, this school of thought, like the explicitly constitutional approaches discussed above, must contend with culturally embedded expectations that make its lessons hard for the public to appreciate.

CONCLUSION

Presidential craft is a derivative, subordinate issue. It asks how a person might best perform a particular job. The nature of the job is determined by reference to the government's creedal values and its operational code. It is also shaped, as we saw in Chapters One, Two, and Three, by the ideas people hold about topics as abstract and diverse as providence, freedom, and power. If craft is mistakenly considered as something more than what it is, there is a risk of distorting our understanding of what the presidency is "about."

An overemphasis on craft might also lead us to misstate the issues involved in reforming the presidency. Some commentators, most notably Theodore Lowi, think that we must reform the presidency so that presidents do not so often fail. My work suggests a different moral: Presidential leadership, especially as it is practiced today, is not impossible but is destructive. Even, or perhaps particularly, when a president, like Reagan, does fulfill (and exploit) the public's expectations of him, we are not made better off as a consequence.

Political science, then, in its elevation of heroic leadership to the status of an empirical and normative model of government, shares responsibility for the immaturity that the public gives evidence of in its relationship to the presidency. But can that relationship be improved upon? Can we overcome fabulism and passivity, the expectation of miracles and the fear that wells within us when miracles do not occur? That we may do so is the hope that lies behind the suggestions that I advance in the next and final chapter.

7

SMASHING THE ICON

Under no form of government is it so dangerous to erect a political idol, as in a democratic republic, for once erected it is the political sin against the Holy Spirit to lay hands upon it. –Von Holst

IF NOT EVERY ICON DESERVES TO BE SMASHED, THE PRESidency is perhaps a leading exception. The preceding chapters provide my answer to the question, Why? Before proceeding to the question, How? I want to restate some of my leading points thus far. To begin with, I acknowledge that some of the ideas by which the people and their presidents are linked are inspiring. Some of them, however, are worthy of criticism in and of themselves, and all of them have had consequences that we could well do without. Let us return briefly, then, to the observations of Chapters One through Six, restating each chapter's subject in the form of a contested axiom of American political culture.

God is on our side. Maybe so, maybe not; political scientists can claim no special insight on this issue. But the belief that ours is a God-favored land has encouraged our presidents to act irresponsibly, at times waging holy war on their political opponents, at other times ignoring problems that might have benefited from more down-to-earth presidential attention.

The president is a crusader for freedom. The belief that presidents should play a central role in expanding freedom similarly puts presidents in a difficult position. The absolutist demands of crusaders for freedom rest on inherently slippery foundations. Even those who press for expansion of freedom do not always want to be confronted with their attendant responsibilities. Prudent presidents permit others to lead in this domain, but our expectation of presidential freedom fighting can make prudence seem like cowardice.

The president is a "strong arm against the world." To escape power, Americans embrace charisma and ritually empower the president to act as their Doppelgänger. The problem, again, is not the idea itself. Some forms of power surely are to be feared. The problem is the consequence of the attempted solution. Charisma is like a spell; while it holds, the charismatic leader is allowed, even encouraged, to commit acts that are then condemned once the spell is broken (and that might never have been attempted had the people not excited the vanity of their leader in the first place).

The president symbolizes America's commitment to democracy. The president may indeed represent our hopes for democracy, but those hopes have some consequences that demand critical attention. Because we have so narrowed the meaning of democracy, every president is now free, even obliged, to claim a democratic mandate that was widely reserved for exceptional presidents of the past.

When extraordinary action is necessary, presidents must take the lead. The bonds of prerogative are exceedingly slack. So long as a president does not act manifestly against the interests of the people, they are likely to defer to his judgment when he claims the mantle of prerogative power. The result is that we often get more than we bargained for from our executives. The people would do well to question more thoroughly a president who claims to be compelled by necessity to employ exceptional powers.

What we need now is presidential leadership! The craft of the presidency, finally, is an important subject. But if we pay attention to how presidents do their job, without inquiring also into the nature of that job, we risk missing the proverbial forest for the trees. What we need now, as a nation, may not be more or even better presidential leadership but rather a new, or at least reconceptualized presidency.

Now, there is nothing wrong with fables, but when they become as attached as they have to one political office, the relationship of the people to the holder of that office suffers as a consequence. The American public is excessively passive before its presidents. For a very large portion of the electorate, presidential politics is not even a spectator sport; it is sheer spectacle.[1] Just over half of the potential electorate now votes in presidential contests, and the long-term trend has been one of decline. Millions of Americans who could vote but do not are nevertheless aware of their presidents. They form opinions about them when asked to do so by pollsters or professors, and they take part in the cultural consumption of the president. They listen to newsclips reporting the details of his life and to talk-show hosts' jokes about his foibles. But they take no active part in presidential politics. The same public is simultaneously excessively demanding of its chief executives. Presidents, even when they are merely watched, are expected to do great things and be great men. When they fail, we fail, and the God-granted destiny of the republic is seemingly jeopardized. Unreasonable hope engenders unreasoning despair. What can a president do, except play his part?

But what if the president's part were to change? Could we, the authors of our presidential drama, rewrite the lead? Perhaps, though it may seem foolish even to try. When social scientists get practical, they risk being proved dead wrong. Furthermore, this book's thesis of a dysfunctional relationship suggests that we approach the subject of change cautiously. A dysfunctional relationship is difficult to change. Both parties to the partnership portrayed in this book are accustomed to their parts. Though an impartial observer can see that the relationship is warped, the people who live it day by day take comfort in their familiar roles. They have become dependent on each other's faults. Despite the difficulties, the relationship of the president with the people seems to me worth the risk of improvement.

CURING A DYSFUNCTIONAL RELATIONSHIP

The first step is to clarify the objective of reform. One fundamental goal of any change in the presidency is well stated by Theodore Lowi. "A good reform," he writes, "would cool if not break up altogether the love affair between the masses and the president."[2] In a more functional relationship, the president and his admirers would not feel the same intensity of kinship as they did, for instance, under Kennedy or Reagan. The collapse of intimacy could, paradoxically, serve another goal. A good reform would strengthen the *political* bond between a president and his supporters. If the symbolic load upon each president's back were made lighter, the people could more readily appraise the president's qualities as a politician. If a postreform president attempted to rally the public to support some extraordinary executive act by invoking the civil religion, or the president's alleged embodiment of the nation, the people would not stir. A postreform president would be a politician, from the beginning of his campaign to the end of his administration. The postreform public would be a citizenry, or at least something closer to that ideal than at present.

If it achieved these two paramount objectives, a good presidential reform would enhance the maturity of the relationship between the president and the people in three ways. First, the balance between passivity and participation would be shifted more heavily toward the latter. Citizens, at the very least, vote. If the stakes in presidential elections were simultaneously less cosmic and more substantive, the urge to participate might be felt among at least some of the millions who now routinely watch but do not act. Second, the public's estimation of the president would be brought down to earth. The president-as-politician would command respect, if he was good at his craft. But he would deserve neither reverence nor contempt, neither love nor hatred. A respected politician, furthermore, would be expected to make policy, not perform miracles. A third consideration follows from the first two. If a president knew he was being evaluated by an engaged citizenry that had adult expectations of his performance, he might well feel free to repay the compliment. The president, that is, might more often "talk turkey" to the people. He would relate bad news as well as good and orient the public's attention toward long-term objectives.

THROUGH A CHANGE IN LAW

Some people immediately think of changing the Constitution when the topic of governmental reform is broached. But changing the Constitution is extremely difficult; a small minority of states can block an amendment. In addition, to a great many Americans, the Constitution is like the presidency; it is a revered part of their national identity. For these reasons, I do not propose addressing the problems of the presidency through constitutional reform. Fortunately, however, constitutional reform is not necessary.

A number of statutory changes could contribute to the objectives set forth above. Statutory changes could go a long way toward depersonalizing the president's role in government. If the president is to be shorn of his imperial robes, he needs to don instead the garments of a party leader. One change in law which could help bring this about would be to introduce proportional representation (PR) in multimember districts to the election of members of the House of Representatives. In PR elections, very few voters need to fear that they will "waste" their ballots if they vote for a candidate without possible plurality appeal. Even with a minority of votes, a candidate can win election in a PR system. Mike Lind, who has made a cogent argument for PR, explains its logic:

> The same hypothetical voting population that, divided into nine single-member districts, now returns nine Democrats, each with a slight plurality in his district, might, if organized into a nine-member district with PR, send four Democrats, three Republicans, one Liberal, and one Conservative to Congress–*with the same votes cast.* . . . Many voters who today are resigned to never electing a congressman of their party or their philosophy, simply because they happen to belong to permanent electoral minorities in their local communities, would suddenly be able to help elect one or more representatives, without changing either their residence or their views.[3]

As a consequence of the adoption of PR, the House, in time, would be divided among more than just two parties. This is where the benefits for the presidency come into view. To understand how this is true requires a brief look at the deficiencies of the current two-party system.

The present party system does not hold the promise of offering voters the sort of choices they once had. Under the two-party system, from roughly 1800 to 1936, America's voters were presented about once each generation with a profound choice between two competing teams of political candidates for national offices. In the choices that voters made at such times, they put into power new partisan teams to direct the government's affairs. Because these "critical elections" were emotionally as well as partisanly charged, the voters stuck with the choices they made. Electoral majorities kept the newly dominant party in control of the presidency, the House, and the Senate for more than a decade after each critical election. Through such elections between the major parties voters sanctioned their government to head in new directions. This occurred in the 1800s, the 1830s, the 1860s, the 1890s, and the 1930s.[4]

Critical realignments of the sort that gave rise to the Civil War and the New Deal—whereby one party was rather abruptly swept out and another brought in and kept there—are now, however, a subject for historians to study. The *partisan* realignment system broke down in the 1960s and is unlikely to be repaired.[5] Rather than promote choice, the present party system magnifies the passivity and personalism of the president-public relationship. Without the occasional rejuvenation that critical realignments once provided, partisanship among the public has become weak. Split-ticket voting has been on the rise now for decades, and even proponents of strengthening the current parties do not deny that they have come to seem irrelevant to a great many Americans.[6]

To decrease the personalism of our national politics, then, we should increase its partisanship. But rather than continue to think of ways to prop up a flagging two-party system, we should consider ways to bring about a more partisan, less personalized multiparty system. PR for House elections is, I think, the most promising potential method. (Waiting for antiparty insurgents like Ross Perot to finish off the two-party system is a distant second choice.) And introducing PR would require nothing more than a change in law, since the Constitution, under Article I, Section 4, grants to Congress the right to determine by law "the times, places, and manner of holding elections for Senators and Representatives."

The benefits to the presidency would not be limited, furthermore, to the indirect benefits of increased partisanship among the electorate. A more direct benefit could derive from the constitutional provision that sends presidential elections to the House if no candidate wins a majority of electoral college votes. This provides a crucial potential link between PR in the House and increased partisan accountability in the presidency. To quote from Theodore Lowi's endorsement of multipartyism:

> The presence of a third [or fourth, or fifth] important party capable of obtaining seats in the House of Representatives and a few electoral votes would hardly throw every presidential election into the House of Representatives. Its presence *would*, however, force each of the candidates for the nomination of the two major parties to look to the House of Representatives as the place where the real election *might take place*. This would transform the presidency because Congress would become the president's direct constituency.[7]

The threat of House elections for the presidency might encourage presidential candidates to seek the backing of multiple-party coalitions. In this way, presidents would be encouraged to view members of Congress as their allies, not opponents. Presidents would perhaps be inhibited in their assertions of executive prerogative, finally, because the public would come to think of the president more as a member of a governing team and less as person in chief of the entire nation.

THROUGH A CHANGE IN CUSTOMS

Customary reform is a necessary complement to statutory changes. Even an American president who governed as a member of a multiparty coalition that represented the interests of an engaged and participatory citizenry would probably never be just another politician in the eyes of the American people. The singularity of his position under the Constitution almost guarantees that the public will be tempted to look to him for guidance. Why not, then, give the president some competition? If, to put it another way, the president's crown can be diminished but not removed, why not award crowns to other political players as well?

Political scientist Donald Robinson has proposed that the president's formal role as head of state be transferred to a national council with important ceremonial responsibilities. Such a council might be filled in one of several ways. It could consist of retired elected officials, or it could be filled by election or by a sort of jury system. If the members were chosen from among former politicians, retired senators, representatives, presidents, vice presidents, justices, and governors might be eligible. Because of their relatively limited number, every living former president and vice president might be a member. The other members could be selected by their currently serving peers in their respective institutions. If chosen by election, federal sponsorship of special elections to fill the council would likely be necessary to encourage those other than the independently wealthy to stand for office. My preference would be to select the members according to principles drawn from both the lottery and the jury.

Consider the following scenario. From the roster of registered voters in each state, twenty potential council members are chosen, purely at random. These twenty then meet under joint federal-state sponsorship to elect two of their number to attend a national council convention. At the national meeting, the one hundred delegates further reduce the membership of their body by election or some combination of lottery and collective choice.

Such a system would, ironically, help to restore the presidency to its constitutional origins. The framers of the Constitution were greatly concerned that the spirit of party might dangerously corrupt the government, including the presidency. After all, how could the head of state simultaneously embody the people and lead a party? How, indeed. The subsequent partisan transformation of the office exacerbated the tension between the president's symbolic and practical roles. The framers were right in their desire to lift the head of state above electioneering; they were wrong, though, to try to remove the head of government from party competition. The head of government's involvement in the party system deserves to be enhanced, but the head of state should not be a partisan post. The proposed system for selecting a plural head of state entirely separate from the presidency would prevent the latter and make the former attainable through means already discussed.

The lottery distributes its benefits without favoritism, which is why it was used in the selection of magistrates in Renaissance Venice and why it had an important role in Michael Harrington's fictional republic, *The Commonwealth of Oceana.*[8] Its proposed use would ensure democratic fairness while eliminating partisan demagoguery from the selection of our "court." The combination of chance with choice, furthermore, would allow for the elevation from the ranks of the randomly chosen of persons with the most prospective talent for symbolic stewardship.

Regardless of how a national council might be chosen, membership should be kept small so that the people might become familiar with their new representatives. They would preside jointly at such events as presidential inaugurations and the opening session of Congress (and the opening of the baseball season). A representative of the Council, not the president, would be granted time on television to console the nation in tragedies and to issue proclamations of thanksgiving. The chairmanship of the council would rotate, preferably by lot. When a foreign head of state was buried, the vice president could stay at home, a member of the council taking his traditional place at the funeral.

In addition, the president deserves some competition in our national heraldry. We celebrate Presidents' Day. Why not celebrate Speakers' Day? How about a Speakers' Memorial in Washington, D.C.? And if Andrew Jackson, the archenemy of paper money, can be made to grace the twenty-dollar bill, surely we should not be timid about proposing that famous Speakers of the House, or senators, also ennoble our currency. The symbols that adorn our money are, after all, more political than we are meant to realize. "In God We Trust" was added to the currency during the Civil War under the authority of the secretary of the treasury, Salmon P. Chase. He was, of course, making a political as well as a theological point. (America's first national coin, the Franklin cent, bore an equally pointed but more secular motto: "Mind Your Business.") Similarly, the Jefferson nickel came into being during the lengthy Franklin Roosevelt administration, as the new Democrats sought to invoke the fame of the first Democrat to legitimate their Hamiltonian revolution in policy.

Even better, perhaps, than a Henry Clay half-dollar, or a Sam Rayburn dime, would be a return to the nineteenth-century practice of using nonpersonal symbols such as Liberty, Mercury, or an Indian war bonnet, though there is a complication to consider. The contemporary difficulty with such motifs is revealed in the choice that the organizers of the Los Angeles Olympics of 1984 made of statues to frame the entrance to the Olympic stadium. On top of the shoulders of two muscular bodies in bronze, one female, one male, stood–absolutely nothing. The statues were headless. If the bodies had had heads, and if the heads had had faces, and if the faces had had racially defining features, some one or two races would have been given an honor withheld from others. In a country still deeply divided over race, just as in the international, interracial Olympic Games, symbolic exclusion is a serious matter. It would perhaps be better, then, to stick with actual persons and invite debate over their selection.

PARTING WORDS

If, after all this, it is nevertheless true, as Oscar Wilde observed, that you cannot "reason someone out of what he has not reasoned himself into," what are the prospects for change in the implausible American presidency?[9] To say that they are probably small is but to underscore the importance of continuing to study the process whereby the American people, over generations and without conscious intent, "decided" to be subjects in a presidential nation. Perhaps a priest-king-democrat is ultimately just the person that the American people desire their president to be; perhaps not. By treating the issue as a matter of choice, in any event, there is much to be learned about the character of the presidency and about the people who perpetuate it in their thoughts.

NOTES

PREFACE

1. Bill Clinton, "A New Covenant," Democratic National Convention, New York City, July 16, 1992, as reprinted in Bill Clinton and Al Gore, *Putting People First: How We Can All Change America* (New York: Times Books, 1992), 226.

2. Perry Miller, *The New England Mind: From Colony to Province* (Boston: Harvard University Press, 1953), 132.

INTRODUCTION

1. See the text of Bush's State of the Union address, *New York Times*, January 30, 1991, A12.

2. This listing is merely illustrative; significant contributions have been made by others. See the citations in later chapters.

3. See Michael Nelson, "Is There a Postmodern Presidency?" *Congress and the Presidency* 16 (Autumn 1989): 155–62.

4. Michael Nelson, "Evaluating the Presidency," in *The Presidency and the Political System*, 2d ed., ed. Michael Nelson (Washington, D.C.: CQ Press, 1988), 5–11.

5. As quoted by Jeffrey Tulis, "The Interpretable Presidency," in Nelson, *The Presidency and the Political System*, 46.

6. Tulis, "Interpretable Presidency," 48.

7. The quotation is from President Lincoln's second annual message to Congress, December 1, 1862, as reprinted in *A Compilation of the Messages and Papers of the Presidents*, comp. James D. Richardson (New York: Bureau of National Literature, 1897), 3343.

8. As quoted by David Hackett Fischer, *Albion's Seed: Four British Folkways in America* (New York: Oxford University Press, 1989), 410.

9. Harvey Mansfield Jr., *Taming the Prince: The Ambivalence of Modern Executive Power* (New York: Free Press, 1989), 284.

10. See James Garfield's inaugural address, March 4, 1881, in Richardson, *Papers of the Presidents*, 4597.

11. John Locke, *Two Treatises of Government*, ed. Peter Laslett (Cambridge: Cambridge University Press, 1988), sec. 160, p. 375.

12. Richard Neustadt, *Presidential Power* (New York: Macmillan, 1960).

1. AMERICA, THE REDEEMER

1. J. L. Magee, "Satan Tempting Booth to the Murder of the President" (Philadelphia, 1865, lithograph), figure 79 in *The Lincoln Image: Abraham Lincoln and the Popular Print*, ed. Harold Holzer, Gabor S. Boritt, and Mark E. Neely Jr. (New York: Charles Scribner's Sons, 1984), 157.

2. Max Rosenthal, "The Last Moments of Abraham Lincoln/President of the United States" (1865), figure 77 in ibid., 154. On Lincoln as Washington's only equal in the popular imagination, see ibid., 203.

3. John Sartain, after a design by W. H. Herman, *Abraham Lincoln the Martyr/Victorious* (New York, 1865), figure 96 in ibid., 197; and see the famous apotheosis scene, D. T. Wiest, "In Memory of Abraham Lincoln–The Reward of the Just" (Philadelphia, 1865), figure 98 in ibid., 200. "Hero, born of woman," is from "The Battle Hymn of the Republic," reprinted and discussed in Ernest Lee Tuveson, *Redeemer Nation: The Idea of America's Millennial Role* (Chicago: University of Chicago Press, 1968), 197–202.

4. Abraham Lincoln, "Address to the New Jersey Senate at Trenton, New Jersey," February 21, 1861, as reprinted in *Abraham Lincoln: Speeches and Writings, 1859–1865*, comp. Don E. Fehrenbacher (New York: Library of America, 1989), 209.

5. "Years of the Modern" (1865), in Walt Whitman, *Leaves of Grass: Authoritative Texts, Prefaces, Whitman on His Art, Criticism*, ed. Sculley Bradley and Harold W. Blodgett (New York: W. W. Norton, 1973), 489–90.

6. George M. Frederickson, *The Inner Civil War: Northern Intellectuals and the Crisis of the Union* (New York: Harper and Row, 1965), 65–66, 71, 120.

7. President Ronald Reagan, paraphrasing Abraham Lincoln, in a speech before the National Association of Evangelicals, Orlando, March 8, 1983, reprinted in Paul D. Erickson, *Reagan Speaks: The Making of an American Myth* (New York: New York University Press, 1985), 157.

8. Tuveson, *Redeemer Nation*, 12. See also Richard V. Pierard and Rob-

ert D. Linder, *Civil Religion and the Presidency* (Grand Rapids, Mich.: Zondervan Publishing House, Academe Books, 1988), 45–48.

9. See David Hackett Fischer, *Albion's Seed: Four British Folkways in America* (New York: Oxford University Press, 1989), 17.

10. Cited in Tuveson, *Redeemer Nation*, 25.

11. From President George Bush's State of the Union address, as reprinted in the *New York Times*, January 30, 1991, A12.

12. As quoted by Pierard and Linder, *Civil Religion and the Presidency*, 27.

13. Conrad Cherry, ed., *God's New Israel: Religious Interpretations of American Destiny* (Englewood Cliffs, N.J.: Prentice-Hall, 1971), 114–15. See also Tuveson, *Redeemer Nation*, 125.

14. Walter Dean Burnham, "The Reagan Heritage," in *The Election of 1988*, ed. Gerald M. Pomper et al. (Chatham, N.J.: Chatham House, 1989), 7.

15. See Robert Bellah, "Civil Religion in America," *Daedalus* 96 (Winter 1967): 1–21.

16. Glenn A. Phelps, "George Washington: Precedent Setter," in *Inventing the American Presidency*, ed. Thomas E. Cronin (Lawrence: University Press of Kansas, 1989), 259–81.

17. Washington, it bears notice, was the first president to proclaim a day of "thanksgiving," when the people of America "may then all unite in rendering unto Him [their] sincere and humble thanks for His kind care and protection of the people of this country." James D. Richardson, comp., *A Compilation of the Messages and Papers of the Presidents* (New York: Bureau of National Literature, 1897), 56 (October 3, 1789).

18. Ibid., 44–45 (April 30, 1789).

19. Cf. Arthur M. Schlesinger Jr., *The Cycles of American History* (Boston: Houghton Mifflin, 1986), ch. 1.

20. Martin Marty, "Two Kinds of Two Kinds of Civil Religion," in *American Civil Religion*, ed. Russell E. Richey and Donald G. Jones (New York: Harper and Row, 1974), 139–57. Cf. H. Mark Roelofs, "The Prophetic President: Charisma in the American Political Tradition," *Polity* 25 (Fall 1992): 1–20.

21. "Reply to Emancipation Memorial Presented by Chicago Christians of All Denominations," September 13, 1862, in *The Collected Works of Abraham Lincoln*, ed. Roy P. Basler, 11 vols. (New Brunswick, N.J.: Rutgers University Press, 1953), 5:420.

22. As Tuveson (*Redeemer Nation*, 205) writes: "We think of the nineteenth century as the period of the triumph of natural science; but it was also the last time in history when many responsible thinkers thought of

human life and history as dominated or at least strongly affected by angels and demons."

23. Second inaugural, delivered March 4, 1865, as reprinted in *An American Primer*, ed. Daniel J. Boorstin (New York: New American Library, 1966), 442–44.

24. Tuveson, *Redeemer Nation*, 207. Lincoln prefigured his second inaugural when he proclaimed a day of thanksgiving, August 12, 1861. See Lincoln's proclamation, reprinted in Basler, *Collected Works*, 4:482.

25. Second inaugural, in Boorstin, *American Primer*, 442–44.

26. As quoted by Boorstin, *American Primer*, 444.

27. David B. Chesebrough, ed. *"God Ordained This War": Sermons on the Sectional Crisis, 1830–1865* (Columbia: University of South Carolina Press, 1991), 27.

28. Richard Hofstadter, *The American Political Tradition and the Men Who Made It* (New York: Vintage Books, 1974), 169.

29. Cited in Holzer, Boritt, and Neely, *Lincoln Image*, 87.

30. Eric Foner and Olivia Mahoney, *A House Divided: America in the Age of Lincoln* (New York: Chicago Historical Society in association with W. W. Norton, 1990), 117–18.

31. *Abraham Lincoln: The Just Magistrate, the Representative Statesman, the Practical Philanthropist*, address by Alex H. Bullock before the city council and citizens of Worcester, June 1, 1865 (Worcester, Mass.: printed by Charles Hamilton).

32. Chesebrough, "*God Ordained This War*," 123.

33. Foner and Mahoney, *House Divided*, 12.

34. Hofstadter, *American Political Tradition*, 159, and see Stephen B. Oates, *With Malice toward None: The Life of Abraham Lincoln* (New York: New American Library, 1977), 432. See also Lincoln's remarks on the New York draft riots in Basler, *Collected Works*, 7:259.

35. "The Eighteenth Presidency! Voice of Walt Whitman to Each Young Man in the Nation, North, South, East, and West," in *Walt Whitman's Workshop: A Collection of Unpublished Manuscripts*, ed. Clifton J. Furness (Cambridge: Harvard University Press, 1928), 102–3.

36. See John Bodnar, *Remaking America: Public Memory, Commemoration, and Patriotism in the Twentieth Century* (Princeton: Princeton University Press, 1992), 35.

37. Ralph Waldo Emerson, "A Plain Man of the People," in Waldo W. Braden, ed., *Building the Myth: Selected Speeches Memorializing Abraham Lincoln* (Urbana: University of Illinois Press, 1990), 30–34.

38. See Eyal J. Naveh, *Crown of Thorns: Political Martyrdom in Ameri-*

ca from Abraham Lincoln to Martin Luther King, Jr. (New York: New York University Press, 1990) 53–58.

39. From Lincoln's annual message to Congress, December 1, 1862, reprinted in Basler, *Collected Works*, 5:537.

40. Address to Confederate veterans, Washington, D.C., June 5, 1917, in *State Papers and Addresses of Woodrow Wilson, President of the United States*, 2d ed., ed. Albert Shaw (New York: George H. Dorman, 1918), 409–10.

41. From a speech Wilson delivered on April 16, 1917, in Shaw, *State Papers*, 392. And see Barry Karl, *The Uneasy State: The United States from 1915 to 1945* (Chicago: University of Chicago Press, 1983), 45.

42. From Wilson's Thanksgiving Proclamation, November 7, 1917, in Shaw, *State Papers*, 433. See also the quotations and discussion in Jan Willem Schulte Nordholt, *Woodrow Wilson: A Life for World Peace* (Berkeley: University of California Press, 1991), 38–46.

43. Ray Stannard Baker and William E. Dodd, eds., *War and Peace: Presidential Messages, Addresses, and Public Papers (1917–1924) by Woodrow Wilson*, 2 vols. (New York: Harper and Brothers, 1927), 2:367.

44. Speech at St. Louis, Missouri, September 5, 1919, in Baker and Dodd, *War and Peace*, 1:645.

45. "Conscience of the world" was Wilson's term for Article X of the league treaty. See Speech at Coliseum, Indianapolis, September 4, 1919, in Baker and Dodd, *War and Peace*, 1:610. The longer quotation is from a speech of September 5, 1919, in ibid., 1:633.

46. See Nordholt, *Woodrow Wilson*, 396.

47. Woodrow Wilson, *Leaders of Men*, edited with an introduction and notes by T. H. Vail Motter (Princeton: Princeton University Press, 1952), 43, 29.

48. John Milton Cooper (*The Warrior and the Priest: Woodrow Wilson and Theodore Roosevelt* [Cambridge: Harvard University Press, 1983], 115, 213, 321–45) is right to insist upon Wilson's pragmatic appreciation of the people's own understanding of their interests. But Cooper, I believe, fails to give sufficient weight to the tremendous edifice of idealism which Wilson sought to create on the basis of a seemingly "realist" foundation.

49. Wilson, *Leaders of Men*, 50.

50. Columbus, Ohio, September 4, 1919, in Baker and Dodd, *War and Peace*, 1:597. See also Nordholt, *Woodrow Wilson*, 46.

51. Wilson, *Leaders of Men*, 50. And see Garry Wills, "The Presbyterian Nietzsche," *New York Review of Books*, January 16, 1992, 3–7.

52. Seattle, Washington, September 13, 1919, in Baker and Dodd, *War and Peace*, 2:194.

53. Ibid. Wilson's words echo Walt Whitman's famous poem of the Civil War, "Beat! Beat! Drums!"

54. See, for example, Nordholt, *Woodrow Wilson*; August Heckscher, *Woodrow Wilson: A Biography* (New York: Charles Scribner's Sons, 1991), 367; and Pierard and Linder, *Civil Religion and the Presidency*, 160.

55. See Robert Kelley, *The Cultural Pattern in American Politics: The First Century* (New York: Alfred A. Knopf, 1979), and John William Ward, *Andrew Jackson: Symbol for an Age* (New York: Oxford University Press, 1953).

56. As quoted by Paul F. Boller, *Presidential Campaigns* (New York: Oxford University Press, 1984), 47.

57. Richardson, *Papers of the Presidents*, 1249–50 (December 3, 1833).

58. Ibid., 1311–12 (April 15, 1834).

59. Ibid., 1527 (March 4, 1837).

60. Ibid., 209–10 (September 17, 1796).

61. Ibid., 45 (April 30, 1789).

62. Ibid., 210–11 (farewell address, September 17, 1796).

63. For a fuller treatment, see Thomas S. Langston, "A Rumor of Sovereignty: The People, Their Presidents, and Civil Religion in the Age of Jackson," *Presidential Studies Quarterly* 23 (Fall 1993): 669–82.

64. "Reverend Reagan," unsigned editorial, *New Republic*, April 4, 1983, reprinted in *Reagan as President: Contemporary Views of the Man, His Politics, and His Policies*, edited with an introduction by Paul Boyer (Chicago: Ivan R. Dee, 1990), 173.

65. Detroit, July 17, 1980, in *Campaign Speeches of American Presidential Candidates, 1948–1984*, ed. Gregory Bush (New York: Frederick Ungar, 1985), 273.

66. See Seymour Martin Lipset, *Continental Divide: The Values and Institutions of the United States and Canada* (New York: Routledge, Chapman and Hall, 1990), 226, and Joel Krieger, *Reagan, Thatcher, and the Politics of Decline* (Cambridge, England: Polity Press, in association with Oxford: Basil Blackwell, 1986).

67. New York, August 14, 1980, in Bush, *Campaign Speeches*, 290, 291.

68. Samuel H. Beer, "In Search of a New Public Philosophy," in *The New American Political System*, ed. Anthony King (Washington, D.C.: American Enterprise Institute, 1978), 43–44.

69. Bruce Miroff, "Ronald Reagan and American Political Culture," *Polity* 20 (Spring 1988): 541. See also Garry Wills, *Reagan's America: Innocents at Home* (New York: Doubleday, 1985).

70. For example, see Reagan's 1984 acceptance speech, delivered on August 23, 1984, in Dallas, reprinted in Bush, *Campaign Speeches*, 318.

71. As quoted in Leland D. Baldwin, *The American Quest for the City of God* (Macon, Ga.: Mercer University Press, 1981), 42. The complete text, in seventeenth-century English, is reprinted in Boorstin, *An American Primer*, 26–43.

72. Erickson, *Reagan Speaks*, 145. Mary Stuckey comments on the passivity of Reagan's rhetoric in *The President as Interpreter-In-Chief* (Chatham, N.J.: Chatham House, 1991), 118–19.

73. Pierard and Linder, *Civil Religion and the Presidency*, 283.

74. See Robert Nisbet, *The Present Age: Progress and Anarchy in Modern America* (New York: Harper and Row, 1988), 29–33, 42–49, 78, 82, 112; Nell Irvin Painter, *Standing at Armageddon: The United States, 1877–1919* (New York: W. W. Norton, 1987), 362–80; and Robert W. Tucker, "Woodrow Wilson, George Bush, and the 'Higher Realism': Brave New World Orders," *New Republic*, February 24, 1992, 24–34.

75. Peter G. Peterson, "Facing Up," *Atlantic Monthly* 272 (October 1993): 78.

76. See, for example, Lawrence Lindsey, *The Growth Experiment: How the New Tax Policy Is Transforming the United States Economy* (New York: Basic Books, 1990), and Paul Craig Roberts, "'Supply-Side' Economics–Theory and Results," *Public Interest* 93 (Fall 1988): 16–36.

77. Bill Clinton, "A New Covenant," Democratic National Convention, New York City, July 16, 1992, as reprinted in Bill Clinton and Al Gore, *Putting People First: How We Can All Change America* (New York: Times Books, 1992), 226.

2. IT'S A FREE COUNTRY

1. Garry Wills, *Lincoln at Gettysburg: The Words That Remade America* (New York: Touchstone/Simon and Schuster, 1992).

2. Frithjof Bergman, *On Being Free* (Notre Dame: University of Notre Dame Press, 1977), 37.

3. From an address at the Sanitary Fair, Baltimore, April 18, 1864, as quoted in *The Political Thought of Abraham Lincoln*, ed. Richard N. Current (Indianapolis: Bobbs-Merrill, 1967), 329.

4. The literature on American individualism is immense. A valuable and highly readable recent work is Robert Bellah et al., *Habits of the Heart: Individualism and Commitment in American Life* (Berkeley: University of California Press, 1985).

5. Berlin's classic essay "Two Concepts of Liberty" is reprinted in

idem, *Four Essays on Liberty* (London: Oxford University Press, 1969), 118–72.

6. See J. David Greenstone, *The Lincoln Persuasion: Remaking American Liberalism* (Princeton: Princeton University Press, 1993).

7. Springfield, Illinois, June 26, 1857, reprinted in Current, *Political Thought*, 88.

8. As quoted by Garry Wills, "The Words That Remade America: Lincoln at Gettysburg," *Atlantic Monthly* 269 (June 1992): 70.

9. Eulogy for Henry Clay, July 6, 1852, in Current, *Political Thought*, 55.

10. First inaugural, in *A Compilation of the Messages and Papers of the Presidents*, comp. James D. Richardson (New York: Bureau of National Literature, 1897), 3213 (March 4, 1861). Lincoln's conciliatory ambitions are emphasized in Robert W. Johannsen, *Lincoln, the South, and Slavery: The Political Dimension* (Baton Rouge: Louisiana State University Press, 1991), 39–40, 56–57.

11. James M. McPherson, *Abraham Lincoln and the Second American Revolution* (New York: Oxford University Press, 1990), 31.

12. George M. Frederickson, *The Inner Civil War: Northern Intellectuals and the Crisis of the Union* (New York: Harper and Row, 1965), 17–19.

13. August 22, 1862, as reprinted in *Abraham Lincoln: A Press Portrait: His Life and Times from the Original Newspaper Documents of the Union, the Confederacy, and Europe*, ed. Herbert Mitgang (1956; Athens, Ga.: University of Georgia Press, 1989), 301.

14. "Reply to Emancipation Memorial Presented by Chicago Christians of All Denominations," September 13, 1862, in *The Collected Works of Abraham Lincoln*, ed. Roy P. Basler, 11 vols. (New Brunswick, N.J.: Rutgers University Press, 1953), 5:420.

15. Veto of Second Confiscation Act, July 17, 1862, reprinted in Current, *Political Thought*, 202. On Lincoln's Whiggery, see David Donald, "Abraham Lincoln: Whig in the White House," in idem, *Lincoln Reconsidered: Essays on the Civil War* (New York: Random House, 1956), ch. 10.

16. "Reply to Emancipation Memorial," 5:424.

17. The Emancipation Proclamation is reprinted with commentary in *An American Primer*, ed. Daniel J. Boorstin (New York: New American Library, 1966), 428–34.

18. Emerson, "The President's Proclamation," *Atlantic Monthly*, November 1862, reprinted in *Lincoln as They Saw Him*, edited and narrated by Herbert Mitgang (New York: Rinehart, 1956), 324.

19. See McPherson, *Abraham Lincoln*, viii, and Philip S. Paludan, "Lincoln and the Rhetoric of Politics," in *A Crisis of Republicanism: American Politics in the Civil War Era*, ed. Lloyd E. Ambrosius (Lincoln: University

of Nebraska Press, 1990), ch. 3. On Lincoln's longing for such an opportunity, see George B. Forgie, *Patricide in the House Divided: A Psychological Interpretation of Lincoln and His Age* (New York: W. W. Norton, 1979).

20. From Lincoln's speech in the summer of 1838 to the Young Men's Lyceum in Springfield, Illinois, reprinted in Current, *Political Thought*, and quoted in Current's introduction, xxx.

21. Message of July 4, 1861, quoted in ibid.

22. Speech on Kansas-Nebraska Act at Peoria, Illinois, October 16, 1854, in Current, *Political Thought*, 73.

23. From final text of the Gettysburg Address, as reprinted in Basler, *Collected Works*, 7:23.

24. McPherson, *Abraham Lincoln*, viii.

25. See Lincoln's second annual message to the Congress, December 1, 1862, in Current, *Political Thought*, 225, 230–32.

26. Speech at Springfield, Illinois, June 26, 1857, in Current, *Political Thought*, 91.

27. "Remarks to a Committee of Colored Men," August 14, 1862, in Current, *Political Thought*, 210.

28. Lincoln's eulogy for Henry Clay, in Current, *Political Thought*, 62.

29. From speech in Peoria, October 16, 1854, in Current, *Political Thought*, 326.

30. Truman, address to the National Association for the Advancement of Colored People (NAACP) at the Lincoln Memorial, June 1947, as quoted by William C. Berman, *The Politics of Civil Rights in the Truman Administration* (Columbus: Ohio State University Press, 1970), 63.

31. From the closing paragraph of Truman's civil rights message, February 2, 1948, in *The Truman Administration: A Documentary History*, ed. Barton J. Bernstein and Allen J. Matusow (New York: Harper and Row, 1966), 107. See also ibid., 114; Donald McCoy and Richard T. Rueteen, *Quest and Response: Minority Rights and the Truman Administration* (Lawrence: University Press of Kansas, 1973), 66, 120; and Truman's *Memoirs of Harry S. Truman*, 2 vols., esp. vol. 2, *Years of Trial and Hope* (Garden City, N.Y.: Doubleday, 1956), 183.

32. See *To Secure These Rights: The Report of the President's Committee on Civil Rights* (Washington, D.C.: United States Government Printing Office, 1947), 23, 38, 88.

33. Barton J. Bernstein, "The Ambiguous Legacy: The Truman Administration and Civil Rights,"in *Politics and Policies of the Truman Administration*, ed. Barton J. Bernstein (Chicago: Quadrangle Books, 1970), 275–76.

34. On the slogan, see Stuart Berg Flexner, *I Hear America Talking: An*

Illustrated History of American Words and Phrases (New York: Touchstone, 1976), 48.

35. William E. Leuchtenburg, "The Conversion of Harry Truman," *American Heritage* (November 1991): 55–68, 56.

36. Executive Order 9809. See Robert J. Donovan, *Conflict and Crisis: The Presidency of Harry Truman, 1945–1948* (New York: W. W. Norton, 1977), 245.

37. *To Secure These Rights.* On the FEPC, see Louis Ruchames, *Race, Jobs, and Politics: The Story of the FEPC* (New York: Columbia University Press, 1952).

38. Harvard Sitkoff, "Harry Truman and the Election of 1948: The Coming of Age of Civil Rights in American Politics," *Journal of Southern History* 37 (November 1971): 597–616.

39. Bernstein, "Ambiguous Legacy," 284.

40. Sitkoff, "Harry Truman," 611.

41. "Crackpot" was Truman's term for Humphrey and company. See David McCullough, *Truman* (New York: Simon and Schuster, 1992), 640.

42. Eugene H. Roseboom, *A History of Presidential Elections: From George Washington to Richard Nixon*, 3d ed. (New York: Macmillan, 1970), 499–500.

43. States' Rights Platform of 1948, in *National Party Platforms, 1840–1956*, comp. Kirk H. Porter and Donald Bruce Johnson (Urbana: University of Illinois Press, 1956), 467.

44. Donovan, *Conflict and Crisis*, 427.

45. See Robert H. Ferrell, *Truman in the White House: The Diary of Eben A. Ayers* (Columbia: University of Missouri Press, 1991), 23–24.

46. Quotation is from Bernstein, "Ambiguous Legacy," 290.

47. McCullough, *Truman*, 590–93.

48. Philip H. Vaughan, *The Truman Administration's Legacy for Black America* (Reseda, Calif.: Mojave Books, 1976), 34.

49. Donovan, *Conflict and Crisis*, 411.

50. See Steven A. Shull, *The President and Civil Rights Policy: Leadership and Change* (New York: Greenwood Press, 1989), 208.

51. October 29, 1948, in *Campaign Speeches of American Presidential Candidates, 1948–1984*, ed. Gregory Bush (New York: Frederick Ungar, 1985), 12.

52. McCullough, *Truman*, 713.

53. Hugh Davis Graham, *The Civil Rights Era: Origins and Development of National Policy* (New York: Oxford University Press, 1990), 16.

54. On Johnson's understanding of politics as the giving of gifts, see

Doris Kearns, *Lyndon Johnson: The American Dream* (New York: Harper and Row, 1976), 54.

55. Robert Dallek illuminates Johnson's liberal nationalism in *Lone Star: Lyndon Johnson and His Times, 1908–1960* (New York: Oxford University Press, 1991), 496, 519.

56. Jack Bass and Walter DeVries, *The Transformation of Southern Politics: Social Change and Political Consequence since 1945* (New York: Basic Books, 1976), 10.

57. George Reedy, *Lyndon B. Johnson: A Memoir* (New York: Andrews and McNeel, 1982), 41.

58. This, at least, is the author's impression of the racial dynamics of the region from which he hails.

59. Merle Miller, *Lyndon: An Oral Biography* (New York: G. P. Putnam's Sons, 1980), 118.

60. See Rowland Evans and Robert Novak, *Lyndon B. Johnson: The Exercise of Power* (New York: New American Library, 1966), ch. 7.

61. Nicholas Lemann, *The Promised Land: The Great Black Migration and How It Changed America* (New York: Alfred A. Knopf, 1991), 115. See also James A. Morone, *The Democratic Wish: Popular Participation and the Limits of American Government* (New York: Basic Books, 1990), 209.

62. Evans and Novak, *Lyndon B. Johnson*, 399.

63. Barry M. Goldwater's acceptance speech, July 17, 1964, in Bush, *Campaign Speeches*, 138–39, 141.

64. Lyndon Johnson's acceptance speech, August 27, 1964, in *A Documentary History of the United States*, 5th ed., ed. Richard D. Heffner (New York: Mentor Books, 1991), 130.

65. Lyndon Baines Johnson, *The Vantage Point: Perspectives on the Presidency, 1963–1969* (New York: Holt, Rinehart, and Winston, 1971), 160.

66. Bass and DeVries, *Transformation of Southern Politics*, 63, 67, but see also 206.

67. Reedy, *Lyndon B. Johnson*, xv.

68. See James Henderson, "The Voting Rights Act of 1965: LBJ and the Department of Justice" (Cambridge: Kennedy School of Government, 1975, Case No. C94-75-114), and Glen Reichardt, "The Voting Rights Act of 1965: Congress and the Voting Rights Act" (Cambridge: Kennedy School of Government, 1975, Case No. C94-75-115).

69. Bass and DeVries, *Transformation of Southern Politics*, 206.

70. Earl Black and Merle Black, *Politics and Society in the South* (Cambridge: Harvard University Press, 1987), 134; and see Mark Stern, *Calculating Visions: Kennedy, Johnson, and Civil Rights* (New Brunswick, N.J.: Rutgers University Press, 1992), 232.

71. Johnson's speech at Howard University, June 4, 1965, in *To Heal and to Build: The Programs of Lyndon B. Johnson*, ed. James McGregor Burns (New York: McGraw Hill, 1968), 219.

72. Ibid., and see also the Voting Rights Act speech, March 15, 1965, in Boorstin, *American Primer*, 951–52.

73. Richard H. King, *Civil Rights and the Idea of Freedom* (New York: Oxford University Press, 1992), 100.

74. As quoted in ibid., 101.

75. See Elijah Muhammad, "An Independent Black Nation and America's Downfall," and Nathan Wright Jr., "Black Power: Self-Development and Self-Respect," as reprinted in *God's New Israel: Religious Interpretations of American Destiny*, ed. Conrad Cherry (Englewood Cliffs, N.J.: Prentice-Hall, 1971), 361–66; 367–75.

76. Cherry, *God's New Israel*, 50–51.

77. Stern, *Calculating Visions*, 229.

78. Benjamin I. Page and Robert Y. Shapiro, *The Rational Public: Fifty Years of Trends in Americans' Policy Preferences* (Chicago: University of Chicago Press, 1992), 62–63, 68–81.

3. TO ESCAPE POWER, EMBRACE CHARISMA

Epigraphs: President Nixon's first inaugural address, "Search for Peace," January 20, 1969, as reprinted in *Vital Speeches of the Day* 35 (February 1, 1969): 227; and John Erlichman, as quoted in Tom Wicker, *One of Us: Richard Nixon and the American Dream* (New York: Random House, 1991), 686.

1. See Theodore J. Lowi, *The Personal President: Power Invested, Promise Unfulfilled* (Ithaca, N.Y.: Cornell University Press, 1985), 115, and Bruce Miroff, "Monopolizing the Public Space: The President as a Problem for Democratic Politics," in *Rethinking the Presidency*, ed. Thomas Cronin (Boston: Little, Brown, 1982), 218–32.

2. The quotations are from Robert E. Lane, *Political Ideology: Why the American Common Man Believes What He Does* (New York: Free Press, 1962).

3. Harvey Mansfield Jr., quoting Machiavelli, in *Taming the Prince: The Ambivalence of Modern Executive Power* (New York: Free Press, 1989), 140.

4. The others, according to Nixon, were John Connally and Nelson Rockefeller. Tom Wicker, *One of Us: Richard Nixon and the American Dream* (New York: Random House, 1991), 544.

5. Richard M. Nixon, acceptance speech, Miami Beach, August 8,

1968, in *Campaign Speeches of American Presidential Candidates, 1948–1984*, ed. Gregory Bush (New York: Frederick Ungar, 1985), 154–55.

6. Paraphrasing Patrick Buchanan, *The New Majority: President Nixon at Mid-Passage* (Philadelphia: Girard National Bank, 1973), 57–58.

7. Allen J. Matusow, *The Unraveling of America: A History of Liberalism in the 1960s* (New York: Harper and Row, 1984), 412–16.

8. Eleanora W. Schoenbaum, *Profiles of an Era: The Nixon-Ford Years* (New York: Harvest/HBJ Books, 1979), 217.

9. Todd Gitlin, *The Sixties: Years of Hope, Days of Rage* (Toronto: Bantam Books, 1987), 346.

10. President Nixon's first inaugural address, January 20, 1969, *Vital Speeches of the Day* 35 (February 1, 1969): 226–27.

11. As quoted by Buchanan, *New Majority*, 9.

12. Richard M. Nixon, "A Vietnam Plan: The Silent Majority," November 3, 1969, reprinted in *Vital Speeches of the Day* 36 (November 15, 1969): 69.

13. George C. Edwards III, with Alec M. Gallup, *Presidential Approval: A Sourcebook* (Baltimore: Johns Hopkins University Press, 1990), 55.

14. Ibid., 53–68. The biggest jump came after the January 27, 1973, signing of an agreement to end the war.

15. Wicker, *One of Us*, 639.

16. Howard F. Stein, "The Silent Complicity of Watergate," *American Scholar* (Winter 1973–74): 21–37.

17. Schoenbaum, *Profiles*, 138, and Colson as quoted in Wicker, *One of Us*, 644.

18. Spurred on by claims that Watergate was a media coup, scholars have exhaustively analyzed coverage of the break-in and the subsequent affair. If the media intended to do Nixon in, their early coverage of Watergate was inexplicably deferential. See James A. Capo, "Network Watergate Coverage Patterns in Late 1972 and Early 1973," *Journalism Quarterly* 60 (Winter 1983): 595–602.

19. Stanley I. Kutler, *The Wars of Watergate: The Last Crisis of Richard Nixon* (New York: Alfred A. Knopf, 1990), 245, citing the papers of Nixon aide John Erlichman.

20. For drawing my attention to Schiller's play, my thanks go to Walter Dean Burnham.

21. Edwards, *Presidential Approval*, 63–65.

22. The answer to the latter question is still debated. Bob Haldeman, Nixon's chief of staff, has asserted that the burglars were looking for evidence linking Larry O'Brien to Howard Hughes, who allegedly had

numerous Washington politicians on his payroll. See Kutler, *Wars of Watergate*, 202.

23. Gladys Engel Lang and Kurt Lang, *The Battle for Public Opinion: The President, the Press, and the Polls during Watergate* (New York: Columbia University Press, 1983), 51.

24. As quoted by Kutler, *Wars of Watergate*, 54.

25. John Locke, *Two Treatises of Government*, ed. Peter Laslett (Cambridge: Cambridge University Press, 1988), 424–25.

26. Senators William S. Cohen and George J. Mitchell, *Men of Zeal: A Candid Inside Story of the Iran-Contra Hearings* (New York: Penguin Books, 1988), xix–xxxii.

27. Nixon's advice is reported in Jane Mayer and Doyle McManus, *Landslide: The Unmaking of the President, 1984–1988* (Boston: Houghton Mifflin, 1988), 307.

28. March 4, 1987, address on the Tower Commission Report, reprinted in *Reagan as President: Contemporary Views of the Man, His Politics, and His Policies*, edited with an introduction by Paul Boyer (Chicago: Ivan R. Dee, 1990), 222.

29. August 12, 1987, address on the Iran-Contra affair, as reprinted in Boyer, *Reagan as President*, 229–30.

30. Roger Rosenblatt, "The Too Personal Presidency," *Time*, November 24, 1986, reprinted in ibid., 233.

31. Haynes Johnson, *Sleepwalking through History: America in the Reagan Years* (New York: W. W. Norton, 1991; New York: Anchor Books, Doubleday, 1992), 153.

32. Edwards, *Presidential Approval*, 132, table 1.7.

33. Ibid., 157, table 3.5, and see Richard A. Brody, *Assessing the President: The Media, Elite Opinion, and Public Support* (Stanford: Stanford University Press, 1991), 41, 87–88.

34. Edwards, *Presidential Approval*, 177–79.

35. Quoted in ibid., 132.

36. Barry Sussman, *What Americans Really Think and Why Our Politicians Pay No Attention* (New York: Pantheon, 1988), 44.

37. Peggy Noonan, *What I Saw at the Revolution: A Political Life in the Reagan Era* (New York: Random House, 1990), 154.

38. This was, of course, the president's campaign slogan in 1984.

39. Daniel Yankelovich and Sidney Harman, *Starting with the People* (Boston: Houghton Mifflin, 1988), 2.

40. Ronald Wilson Reagan, *Ronald Reagan: An American Life* (New York: Simon and Schuster, 1990), 532.

41. As reported in Mayer and McManus, *Landslide*, 358.

42. Johnson, *Sleepwalking*, 361.

43. Cohen and Mitchell, *Men of Zeal*, 157.

44. As recounted in ibid., 363.

45. James W. Ceaser, "The Reagan Presidency and American Public Opinion," in *The Reagan Legacy: Promise and Performance*, ed. Charles Jones (Chatham, N.J.: Chatham House, 1988), 202.

4. THE PRESIDENT IS OUR PROPERTY

1. Clinton Rossiter, ed., *The Federalist Papers* (New York: New American Library, 1961), 387.

2. Joshua Miller, "The Ghostly Body Politic: The Federalist Papers and Popular Sovereignty," *Political Theory* 16 (Fall 1988): 104. For a more measured and detailed analysis of the topic, see Edmund S. Morgan, *Inventing the People: The Rise of Popular Sovereignty in England and America* (New York: W. W. Norton, 1988).

3. Rossiter, *Federalist Papers*, 387.

4. Sir William A. Craige and James R. Hulbert, eds., *A Dictionary of American English on Historical Principles* (Chicago: University of Chicago Press, 1940), 744–45. Charles Maier suggests that this usage was temporarily delegitimated by the "Democratic Societies" of the 1790s, alleged by President Washington to have plotted the Whiskey Rebellion. See Charles S. Maier, "Democracy since the French Revolution," in *Democracy: The Unfinished Journey, 508 BC to AD 1993*, ed. John Dunn (Oxford: Oxford University Press, 1992), 125.

5. In a way, this was a return to etymological roots. The origins of the word *democracy* are in the Greek suffix meaning "rule" and the Greek word *demos*, which denoted the people of a certain nonelite district, and plain people more generally.

6. From the Gettysburg Address. Lincoln adapted the phrase from Theodore Parker, who in 1850 defined democracy in an abolitionist speech as "a government of all the people, by all the people, for all the people." See William Safire, *Safire's Political Dictionary* (New York: Random House, 1978), 319–20.

7. Abraham Lincoln, boasting in 1858 of the Republican's success in attracting "much of the plain old Democracy" but almost none of "the nice exclusive sort." As quoted in Richard Hofstadter, *The American Political Tradition and the Men Who Made It* (New York: Vintage Books, 1974), 100.

8. Andrew Carnegie, *Triumphant Democracy or Fifty Years' March of the Republic* (New York: Charles Scribner's Sons, 1888), 394.

9. First inaugural, March 4, 1861, as quoted by Robert Dahl, *A Preface to Democratic Theory* (Chicago: University of Chicago Press, 1956), 35.

10. As quoted in ibid.

11. National Endowment for Democracy 1992 Annual Report, 103d Cong., 1st sess. (Washington: United States Government Printing Office, 1993), 6.

12. Russell L. Hanson, *The Democratic Imagination in America* (Princeton: Princeton University Press, 1985), 258. And see idem, "Democracy," in *Political Innovation and Conceptual Change*, ed. Terrence Ball, James Farr, and Russell L. Hanson (Cambridge: Cambridge University Press, 1989), 68–89.

13. James Sterling Young, *The Washington Community, 1800–1828* (New York: Harcourt, Brace, Jovanovich, 1966), 240–41.

14. James D. Richardson, comp., *A Compilation of the Messages and Papers of the Presidents* (New York: Bureau of National Literature, 1897), 1152. In the remainder of this chapter, this series is cited parenthetically in the text as "*CMPP*."

15. Calvin Colton, ed., *The Works of Henry Clay*, 7 vols. (New York: G. P. Putnam's Sons, 1904), 5:576–77.

16. Robert V. Remini, *The Election of Andrew Jackson* (Philadelphia: J. B. Lippincott, 1963), 192.

17. See Charles Sellers, *The Market Revolution: Jacksonian America, 1815–1846* (New York: Oxford University Press, 1992), and Aaron Wildavsky, "Resolved, That Individualism and Egalitarianism Be Made Compatible in America: Political-Cultural Roots of Exceptionalism," in *Is America Different? A New Look at American Exceptionalism*, ed. Byron Shafer (Oxford: Clarendon Press, 1991), ch. 5.

18. See Richard Ellis and Aaron Wildavsky, *Dilemmas of Presidential Leadership* (New Brunswick, N.J.: Transaction Press, 1989), ch. 6; Robert Kelley, *The Cultural Pattern in American Politics: The First Century* (New York: Alfred A. Knopf, 1979), chs. 5 and 6; David Hackett Fischer, *Albion's Seed: Four British Folkways in America* (New York: Oxford University Press, 1989), 847–50; and Lee Benson, *The Concept of Jacksonian Democracy: New York as a Test Case* (Princeton: Princeton University Press, 1961), esp. ch. 5.

19. As reprinted in *The Meaning of Jacksonian Democracy*, ed. Edwin C. Rozwenc (Boston: D. C. Heath, 1963), 19, 21.

20. Kirk H. Porter and Donald Bruce Johnson, comps., *National Party Platforms, 1840–1956* (Urbana: University of Illinois Press, 1956), 3.

21. George Bancroft, "The Office of the People in Art, Government, and

Religion," an oration delivered at Williams College in 1835. Reprinted in Rozwenc, *Meaning of Jacksonian Democracy*, 16–17.

22. From the *Review*'s opening editorial, as reprinted in Rozwenc, *Meaning of Jacksonian Democracy*, 19.

23. Porter and Johnson, *National Party Platforms*.

24. G. Scott Thomas, *The Pursuit of the White House: A Handbook of Presidential Election Statistics and History* (Westport, Conn.: Greenwood Press, 1987), 20.

25. Eugene H. Roseboom, *A History of Presidential Elections: From George Washington to Richard Nixon*, 3d ed. (New York: Macmillan, 1970), 104.

26. James Parton, *Life of Andrew Jackson*, 3 vols. (New York: Mason Brothers, 1860), 3:420–24, and Robert V. Remini, *Andrew Jackson and the Course of American Empire*, 3 vols. (New York: Harper and Row, 1977–84), vol. 2, *Andrew Jackson and the Course of American Freedom, 1822–1832* (1981), 375–76.

27. Roger A. Fischer, *Tippecanoe and Trinkets Too: The Material Culture of American Presidential Campaigns* (Urbana: University of Illinois Press, 1988), 16–18, and Joseph Bucklin Bishop, *Our Political Drama: Conventions, Campaigns, Candidates* (New York: Scott-Thomas, 1904), 104–17.

28. Richard P. McCormick, *The Presidential Game: The Origins of American Presidential Politics* (New York: Oxford University Press, 1982), 154.

29. See the contrasting analyses of Joel H. Silbey, "Beyond Realignment and Realignment Theory: American Political Eras, 1789–1989," and Walter Dean Burnham, "Critical Realignment: Dead or Alive?" both in *The End of Realignment? Interpreting American Electoral Eras*, ed. Byron E. Shafer (Madison: University of Wisconsin Press, 1991), 3–23, 101–40.

30. Michael Nelson, "A Short, Ironic History of Bureaucracy," *Journal of Politics* (August 1982): 759; cf. Harry Watson, *Liberty and Power: The Politics of Jacksonian America* (New York: Hill and Wang, 1990), 103–4.

31. For Jackson's own argument along these lines, see his inaugural address, in Richardson, *Papers of the Presidents*, 1001.

32. See Stephen Skowronek, *Building a New American State: The Expansion of National Administrative Capacities, 1877–1920* (Cambridge: Cambridge University Press, 1982), 25.

33. James A. Morone, *The Democratic Wish: Popular Participation and the Limits of American Government* (New York: Basic Books, 1990), 92–93. And see Nelson, "Short, Ironic History," 761–63.

34. Marcus Cunliffe, *The Presidency* (Boston: Houghton Mifflin, 1987),

112, and Richard Hofstadter, *The Idea of a Party System: The Rise of Legitimate Opposition in the United States, 1780–1840* (Berkeley: University of California Press, 1969), 247–48.

35. Alexis de Tocqueville, *Democracy in America*, 2 vols. (New York: Alfred A. Knopf, 1945) 1:56.

36. Ellis and Wildavsky, *Dilemmas*, 116–18.

37. For a contrary assessment, see Hanson, *Democratic Imagination*, 131–36. See also Robert Shalhope, "Republicanism in Early American Historiography," *William and Mary Quarterly* 39 (April 1982): 342, 347–49.

38. Jeffrey K. Tulis, *The Rhetorical Presidency* (Princeton: Princeton University Press, 1987), 96–97, 106–16.

39. M. J. Heale, *The Presidential Quest: Candidates and Images in American Political Culture, 1789–1852* (London: Longman College, 1982), 90.

40. Gil Troy, *See How They Ran: The Changing Role of the Presidential Candidate* (New York: Free Press, 1991), caption to an illustration between pp. 116 and 117. Troy makes this statement in reference to the 1840s. His own work suggests its applicability to the century as a whole.

41. Herbert Croly, *The Promise of American Life* (New York: Macmillan, 1909), 47, 69, 126, 207, 270; and see Walter E. Weyl, *The New Democracy: An Essay on Certain Economic and Political Tendencies in the United States* (New York: Macmillan, 1912).

42. George Record, in a letter to President Wilson, as quoted by Hofstadter, *American Political Tradition*, 360.

43. Gordon Wood, *The Radicalism of the American Revolution* (New York: Alfred A. Knopf, 1992), 234.

44. William Howard Taft, *Our Chief Magistrate and His Powers* (New York: Columbia University Press, 1916), 139–57.

45. See Richard E. Neustadt, *Presidential Power and the Modern Presidents: The Politics of Leadership from Roosevelt to Reagan* (New York: Free Press, 1990), 4–6, and William E. Leuchtenburg, *In the Shadow of FDR: From Harry Truman to Ronald Reagan* (Ithaca, N.Y.: Cornell University Press, 1983).

46. Edward Jay Epstein, "The Second Coming of Jim Garrison," *Atlantic Monthly* (March 1993): 94.

47. Garry Wills, *The Kennedy Imprisonment: A Meditation on Power* (Boston: Little, Brown, 1981).

48. Norman Mailer, "Superman Comes to the Supermarket," reprinted in idem, *The Presidential Papers* (New York: Berkley Medallion Books, 1963), 39. Wills cites the same passage in *Kennedy Imprisonment*, 283.

49. Wills, *Kennedy Imprisonment*, 34.

50. Troy, *See How They Ran*, 208.

51. Irwin Silber, *Songs America Voted By* (Harrisburg, Pa.: Stackpole Books, 1988), 294–95.

52. See Gerald Gardner, *The Mocking of the President: A History of Campaign Humor from Ike to Ronnie* (Detroit: Wayne State University Press, 1988).

53. Bruce Miroff, *Pragmatic Illusions: The Presidential Politics of John F. Kennedy* (New York: Longman, 1976), 13–18.

54. Marquis James, *The Life of Andrew Jackson* (Indianapolis: Bobbs-Merrill, 1938), 508.

55. Paul F. Boller Jr., *Presidential Anecdotes* (New York: Oxford University Press, 1981), 80–81.

56. James, *Life of Andrew Jackson*, 519.

5. THE PEOPLE RESPOND TO PRESIDENTIAL PREROGATIVE

1. This is a paraphrase of John Locke, *Two Treatises of Government*, ed. Peter Laslett (Cambridge: Cambridge University Press, 1988), 375.

2. Some commentators see the constitutional basis of prerogative differently, tracing it to the Constitution's text rather than to the structural properties of the government that it created. For an elaboration of my view, see Thomas S. Langston and Michael E. Lind, "John Locke and the Limits of Presidential Prerogative," *Polity* 24 (Fall 1991): 49–68.

3. Clinton Rossiter, ed., *The Federalist Papers* (New York: New American Library, 1961), 424. See also Jeffrey K. Tulis, "The Constitutional Presidency in American Political Development," in *The Constitution and the American Presidency*, ed. Martin Fausold and Alan Shank (Albany: State University of New York Press, 1991), 139–41.

4. Robert S. Hirschfield, *The Constitution and the Court: The Development of the Basic Law through Judicial Interpretation* (New York: Random House, 1962), 138.

5. James G. Randall, *Constitutional Problems under Lincoln* (Urbana: University of Illinois Press, 1964), esp. 118–39.

6. Arthur M. Schlesinger Jr., *The Imperial Presidency* (Boston: Houghton Mifflin, 1973), 69.

7. Hirschfield, *Constitution and the Court*, 145.

8. Christopher H. Pyle and Richard M. Pious, *The President, Congress, and the Constitution: Power and Legitimacy in American Politics* (New York: Free Press, 1984), 235–39.

9. Harold Hongju Koh, *The National Security Constitution: Sharing*

Power after the Iran-Contra Affair (New Haven: Yale University Press, 1990), 94.

10. Hirschfield, *Constitution and the Court*, 166.

11. Edward S. Corwin, *The President: Office and Powers, 1787–1984*, 5th ed., revised by Randall W. Bland, Theodore T. Hindson, and Jack W. Peltason (New York: New York University Press, 1984), 291.

12. David McCullough, *Truman* (New York: Simon and Schuster, 1992), 898.

13. Ibid., and see Hirschfield, *Constitution and the Court*, 170–71.

14. Harry S. Truman, *Memoirs of Harry S. Truman*, vol. 2, *Years of Trial and Hope* (Garden City, N.Y.: Doubleday, 1956), 476.

15. McCullough, *Truman*, 897.

16. Hirschfield, *Constitution and the Court*, 185.

17. Truman, *Memoirs*, 2:470.

18. Richard M. Pious, *The American Presidency* (New York: Basic Books, 1979), 66.

19. Justice Hugo Black delivered the opinion of the Court; the five other justices in the majority each issued a separate concurrence. For excerpts, see Pyle and Pious, *President, Congress, and the Constitution*, 125–38.

20. Bert Cochran, *Harry Truman and the Crisis Presidency* (New York: Funk and Wagnalls, 1973), 344.

21. Locke, *Two Treatises*, 376.

22. I rely here on Terry Eastland, *Energy in the Executive: The Case for the Strong Presidency* (New York: Free Press, 1992), 126–30.

23. As excerpted in Pyle and Pious, *President, Congress, and the Constitution*, 362–63.

24. Eastland, *Energy in the Executive*, 136.

25. U.S. News and World Report, *Triumph without Victory: The Unreported History of the Persian Gulf War* (New York: Times Books/Random House, 1992), ix. For a richly detailed history of the war, see Dilip Hiro, *Desert Shield to Desert Storm: The Second Gulf War* (New York: Harper Collins, 1992). For an overview of the war which focuses on President Bush's decision making, see Jean Edward Smith, *George Bush's War* (New York: Henry Holt, 1992).

26. Locke, *Two Treatises*, 375.

27. George C. Edwards III, with Alec M. Gallup, *Presidential Approval: A Sourcebook* (Baltimore: Johns Hopkins University Press, 1990), 146.

28. *Oxford English Dictionary*, 2d ed. (Oxford: Clarendon Press, 1991).

29. Quoted in Charles C. Thach Jr., *The Creation of the Presidency*,

1775–1789: A Study in Constitutional History (1992; New York: Da Capo Press, 1969), 101.

30. Robert E. DiClerico, *The American Presidency* (Englewood Cliffs, N.J.: Prentice-Hall, 1990), 338–39.

31. Theodore Roosevelt, *An Autobiography* (New York: Macmillan, 1916), 563. John Morton Blum, *The Progressive Presidents: Theodore Roosevelt, Woodrow Wilson, Franklin D. Roosevelt, Lyndon B. Johnson* (New York: W. W. Norton, 1980), 57.

32. See Jefferson's letter to Spencer Roane, September 6, 1819, in *The Writings of Thomas Jefferson*, 10 vols., ed. Paul Leicester Ford (New York: G. P. Putnam's Sons, 1892–99), 10:140.

33. Forrest McDonald, *The Presidency of Thomas Jefferson* (Lawrence: University Press of Kansas, 1976), 69.

34. Robert W. Tucker and David C. Hendrickson, *Empire of Liberty: The Statecraft of Thomas Jefferson* (New York: Oxford University Press, 1990), 32.

35. As quoted in ibid., 94.

36. Jefferson to John Dickinson, August 9, 1803, as quoted in Everett Somerville Brown, *The Constitutional History of the Louisiana Purchase, 1803–1812* (Berkeley: University of California Press, 1920), 23.

37. Ford, *Writings of Thomas Jefferson*, 8:241 n.

38. As quoted by Brown, *Constitutional History*, 25.

39. James D. Richardson, comp., *A Compilation of Messages and Papers of the Presidents* (New York: Bureau of National Literature, 1897), 346, 348.

40. As quoted in Alexander DeConde, *This Affair of Louisiana* (Baton Rouge: Louisiana State University Press, 1976), 192.

41. Jefferson, in a letter to Horatio Gates, complained of this tendency. See Jefferson to Gates, July 11, 1803, in Ford, *Writings of Thomas Jefferson*, 8:249.

42. As quoted by McDonald, *Presidency of Thomas Jefferson*, 71.

43. Tucker and Hendrickson, *Empire of Liberty*, 312–13 n. 166.

44. Lincoln's special session message, July 4, 1861, as reprinted in Richardson, *Papers of the Presidents*, 3224.

45. Randall, *Constitutional Problems*, 34–41.

46. Richardson, *Papers of the Presidents*, 3257.

47. His actions, Lincoln at one point stated to the Congress, "whether strictly legal or not, were ventured upon under what appeared to be a popular demand and a public necessity." As quoted by Pyle and Pious, *President, Congress, and the Constitution*, 323.

48. Raoul Berger, "War-Making by the President," *University of Pennsylvania Law Review* 121 (1972): 64.

49. Pious, *American Presidency*, 58.

50. Letter to Albert G. Hodges, April 4, 1864, as reprinted in Pyle and Pious, *President, Congress, and the Constitution*, 65.

51. Pious, *American Presidency*, 56–57.

52. Randall, *Constitutional Problems under Lincoln*, xxvi.

53. Pious, *American Presidency*, 54.

54. From Roosevelt's inaugural, as reprinted in *An American Primer*, ed. Daniel J. Boorstin (New York: New American Library, 1985), 868.

55. Quoted in Arthur M. Schlesinger Jr., *The Coming of the New Deal* (Boston: Houghton Mifflin, 1958), 1.

56. Theodore J. Lowi, *The Personal President: Power Invested, Promise Unfulfilled* (Ithaca, N.Y.: Cornell University Press, 1985), 46.

57. As reprinted in Boorstin, *An American Primer*, 867.

58. Rexford Guy Tugwell, *The Industrial Discipline and the Governmental Arts* (New York: Columbia University Press, 1933), 218.

59. Rexford Guy Tugwell, *Roosevelt's Revolution: The First Year, a Personal Perspective* (New York: Macmillan, 1977), 145.

60. As quoted and discussed in Thomas S. Langston, *Ideologues and Presidents: From the New Deal to the Reagan Revolution* (Baltimore: Johns Hopkins University Press, 1992), 30.

61. Robert Eden, "On the Origins of the Regime of Pragmatic Liberalism: John Dewey, Adolf A. Berle, and FDR's Commonwealth Club Address," *Studies in American Political Development* 7 (Spring 1993): 107.

62. Ibid., 109. And consider Roosevelt's remarks to some farmers of the Tennessee Valley. The New Deal, he said, meant that the "kind of rugged individualism that allows an individual to do this, that, or the other thing that will hurt his neighbors" is gone forever. "He is forbidden to do that from now on." *Public Papers and Addresses of Franklin Roosevelt*, 13 vols., comp. Samuel Rosenman (New York: Random House, 1938–50), 3:462.

63. As quoted in Eden, "On the Origins of the Regime of Pragmatic Liberalism," 124.

64. Lester G. Seligman and Elmer E. Cornwell Jr., *New Deal Mosaic: Roosevelt Confers with His National Emergency Council, 1933–1936* (Eugene: University of Oregon, 1965), 75.

65. Blum, *Progressive Presidents*, 89.

6. WANTED: HEROES IN THE WHITE HOUSE

1. Edmund S. Morgan, *Inventing the People: The Rise of Popular Sovereignty in England and America* (New York: W. W. Norton, 1988), 305.

2. Clinton Rossiter, ed., *The Federalist Papers* (New York: New American Library, 1961), 432.

3. On Washington, see Daniel J. Boorstin, *The Americans: The National Experience* (New York: Random House, 1965), 337–56, and David Curtis Skaggs, "George Washington," in *Popular Images of American Presidents*, ed. William C. Spragens (New York: Greenwood Press, 1988), 1–26. On Adams, see Bruce Miroff, "John Adams and the Presidency," in *Inventing the American Presidency*, ed. Thomas E. Cronin (Lawrence: University Press of Kansas, 1989), 304–25. On Jefferson, see Ronald L. Hatzenbuehler, "Thomas Jefferson," in Spragens, *Popular Images*, 27–45.

4. See generally Edward Pessen, *The Log-Cabin Myth: The Social Backgrounds of the Presidents* (New Haven: Yale University Press, 1984), and Gary Boyd Roberts, comp., *Ancestors of American Presidents* (Santa Clarita, Calif.: Boyer, 1989).

5. See Gil Troy, *See How They Ran: The Changing Role of the Presidential Candidate* (New York: Free Press, 1991), 105–6.

6. Robert K. Carr, "Out of a Great Office, Greatness: Two New Studies Illuminate the Role and Powers of Our Chief Executive," *New York Times*, May 13, 1956, review of Edward S. Corwin and Louis W. Koenig, *The Presidency Today* (New York: New York University Press, 1956), and Clinton Rossiter, *The American Presidency* (New York: Harcourt, Brace, 1956), as reprinted in *The Great Contemporary Issues: The Presidency*, ed. Joanne Soderman and George Reedy (New York: Arno Press, 1975), 32–33.

7. Tom Wicker, "Politicians Preferred," *New York Times*, December 18, 1960, review of Richard Neustadt, *Presidential Power: The Politics of Leadership* (New York: John Wiley and Sons, 1960), and *The Ultimate Decision: The President as Commander in Chief*, ed. Ernest R. May (New York: George Brazilier, 1960), reprinted in Soderman and Reedy, *Great Contemporary Issues*, 35.

8. *Goals for Americans: The Report of the President's Commission on National Goals* (New York: Prentice-Hall, Spectrum Books, 1960), xi.

9. Fred Greenstein, *The Hidden-Hand Presidency: Eisenhower as Leader* (New York: Basic Books, 1982; reprint, Baltimore: Johns Hopkins University Press, 1994).

10. The remaining two schools, which are considerably newer than the other four, are the historical and the cultural. Because their practical impact on how presidents and the public think about leadership has thus

far been slight, I do not discuss them here. The historical school is ably represented by Stephen Skowronek, *The Politics Presidents Make: Leadership from John Adams to George Bush* (Cambridge: Harvard University Press, 1993), and Erwin Hargrove and Michael Nelson, *Presidents, Politics, and Policy* (Baltimore: Johns Hopkins University Press, 1984). A cultural perspective is offered by Richard Ellis and Aaron Wildavsky, *Dilemmas of Presidential Leadership* (New Brunswick, N.J.: Transaction Press, 1989).

11. Richard E. Neustadt, commenting on his course on the presidency. David Shribman, "Harvard Professor's Course Has Shaped Views of a Generation on the Power of the Presidency," *Wall Street Journal*, December 4, 1986, 68. The most recent version of the text is Richard Neustadt, *Presidential Power and the Modern Presidents: The Politics of Leadership from Roosevelt to Reagan* (New York: Free Press, 1990).

12. *Presidential Power and the Modern Presidents*, xx–xxi.

13. Thomas E. Cronin, *The State of the Presidency* (Boston: Little, Brown, 1975), 29.

14. *Presidential Power and the Modern Presidents*, xix.

15. Arthur M. Schlesinger Jr. uses the phrase repeatedly in *The Crisis of Confidence* (Boston: Houghton Mifflin, 1967). For detailed treatment of Democratic party liberalism as an ideology, see my book *Ideologues and Presidents: From the New Deal to the Reagan Revolution* (Baltimore: Johns Hopkins University Press, 1992).

16. James McGregor Burns, *Leadership* (New York: Harper and Row, 1978), 389.

17. James McGregor Burns, *The Power to Lead: The Crisis of the American Presidency* (New York: Simon and Schuster, 1984), 16.

18. James David Barber, *Presidential Character: Predicting Performance in the White House*, 4th ed. (Englewood Cliffs, N.J.: Prentice-Hall, 1992).

19. Terry Eastland, *Energy in the Executive: The Case for the Strong Presidency* (New York: Free Press, 1992), 10.

20. Jeffrey K. Tulis, *The Rhetorical Presidency* (Princeton: Princeton University Press, 1987).

21. Ibid., 195, and Eastland, *Energy in the Executive*, ch. 2.

22. Tulis, *Rhetorical Presidency*, 22.

23. Richard M. Pious, *The American Presidency* (New York: Basic Books, 1979).

24. Theodore J. Lowi, "Afterword: The Paradox of Presidential Power," in *The Constitution and the American Presidency*, ed. Martin Fausold

and Alan Shank (Albany: State University of New York Press, 1991), 240–41.

25. Theodore J. Lowi, *The Personal President: Power Invested, Promise Unfulfilled* (Ithaca, N.Y.: Cornell University Press, 1985), 176–212.

26. Shribman, "Harvard Professor's Course," 68.

27. Richard E. Neustadt, "Memorandum on Staffing the President-Elect," October 30, 1960, as reprinted in *The Managerial Presidency*, ed. James P. Pfiffner (Pacific Grove, Calif.: Brooks/Cole, 1991), 28.

28. Neustadt, *Presidential Power and the Modern Presidents*, 127.

29. See Charles O. Jones, *The Trusteeship Presidency: Jimmy Carter and the United States Congress* (Baton Rouge: Louisiana State University Press, 1988), and Wynne Walker Moskop, "Prudence as a Critique of Presidential Leadership Theory," paper prepared for delivery at the annual meeting of the American Political Science Association, Washington, D.C., September 1991, 14–15, 22–25.

30. Barber, *Presidential Character*, 398–400, 430–33.

31. See Bert Rockman, "What Didn't We Know, and Should We Forget It?" *Polity* 21 (Summer 1989): 777–92.

32. In 1933, writers—perhaps in fear of the Napoleonic echoes of a Hundred Days of rulership—celebrated the first *ninety-nine* days of the administration. Some time later, another day was added. See *The World's Greatest Ninety-Nine Days scissored and pasted by Ben Duffy and Harford Powell*, comp. Ben Duffy and Harford Willing Hare (New York: Harper and Brothers, 1933).

33. See my *Ideologues and Presidents*, 183.

34. Lowi, *Personal President*, 212.

35. See Nelson W. Polsby, "Against Presidential Greatness," *Commentary* (January 1977): 61–64.

36. See Aaron Friedberg, "Why Didn't the United States Become a Garrison State?" *International Security* 16 (Spring 1992): 109–42.

37. See Melanie Billings-Yun, *Decision against War: Eisenhower and Dien Bien Phu, 1954* (New York: Columbia University Press, 1988), and Greenstein, *Hidden-Hand Presidency*.

38. See Arthur M. Schlesinger Jr., "The Cycles of American Politics," in idem, *The Cycles of American History* (Boston: Houghton Mifflin, 1986), ch. 2.

39. Hargrove and Nelson, *Presidents, Politics, and Policy*, and Skowronek, *Politics Presidents Make*. See also Bert Rockman, *The Leadership Question: The Presidency and the American System* (New York: Praeger, 1984), ch. 4.

7. SMASHING THE ICON

1. Bruce Miroff usefully defines presidential spectacle as "the utilization of modern media, especially television, to present the president in visible and highly dramatic actions designed to establish a favorable public identity [and] that minimize the potential for public interruption and treat citizens as passive spectators." Bruce Miroff, "Secrecy and Spectacle: Reflections on the Dangers of the Presidency," in *The Presidency in American Politics*, ed. Paul Brace, Christine B. Harrington, and Gary King (New York: New York University Press, 1989), 157.

2. Theodore J. Lowi, *The Personal President: Power Invested, Promise Unfulfilled* (Ithaca, N.Y.: Cornell University Press, 1985), 183.

3. Michael Lind, "A Radical Plan to Change American Politics," *Atlantic Monthly* (August 1992): 76–77.

4. See Walter Dean Burnham, *Critical Elections and the Mainsprings of American Politics* (New York: W. W. Norton, 1970).

5. On the old-time partisan realignment and what might be replacing it, see my *Ideologues and Presidents: From the New Deal to the Reagan Revolution* (Baltimore: Johns Hopkins University Press, 1992). See also *The End of Realignment? Interpreting American Electoral Eras*, ed. Byron E. Shafer (Madison: University of Wisconsin Press, 1991).

6. Larry Sabato, *The Party's Just Begun: Shaping Political Parties for America's Future* (Glenview, Ill.: Scott, Foresman, 1988), and David Price, *Bringing Back the Parties* (Washington, D.C.: CQ Press, 1985). See also Martin Wattenberg, *The Decline of American Political Parties, 1952–1992* (Cambridge: Harvard University Press, 1994).

7. Lowi, *Personal President*, as quoted by Lind, "A Radical Plan," 82.

8. See Robert Finlay, *Politics in Renaissance Venice* (New Brunswick, N.J.: Rutgers University Press, 1980), and Donald L. Robinson, *To the Best of My Ability: The Presidency and the Constitution* (New York: W. W. Norton, 1987), 20–22.

9. As quoted by John Patrick Diggins, *The Lost Soul of American Politics: Virtue, Self-Interest, and the Foundations of Liberalism* (New York: Basic Books, 1984), 3.

INDEX

Library of Congress Cataloging-in-Publication Data

Langston, Thomas S.
With reverence and contempt :
how Americans think about their president /
Thomas S. Langston.
p. cm. – (Interpreting American politics)
Includes bibliographical references and index.
ISBN 0-8018-5016-9 (alk. paper).
1. Presidents–United States–History. 2. Presidents–United States–Public opinion. 3. Public opinion–United States. I. Title. II. Series.
JK511.L36 1995
353.03'13–dc20 94-34134